# At
# with the
# Inner Self

## Jim Burns

TAT Foundation Press

Published by TAT Foundation Press
47 Washington Avenue #150
Wheeling, West Virginia 26003
www.tatfoundation.org

Text font: Palatino Linotype

Main entry under title: *At Home with the Inner
Self*

1. Spirituality          2. Psychology

Library of Congress control number:
2011933948


ISBN: 978-0-9799630-7-0

Interior photos: B. Erne – p. 30, 56, and 94
         Art Ticknor – p. 8, 12, 22, 66, and 108
         Dan Mottsman – p. 118
Cover design: Bob Fergeson
Layout: Shawn Nevins

# Contents

# Foreword

Imagine knowing a flame held to your hand is not real, yet it burns. Such is a thought I've had as I sat and listened to Jim Burns over the years. One minute angrily denouncing the torments inflicted upon him by his father and threatening to beat God with a baseball bat, and the next espousing a complete faith in the capacity of one's inner self to solve all of our problems.

Others know him better, yet it has fallen to me to write about a man I scarcely understood at the time I needed his help the most. Jim Burns was the only living person that Richard Rose spoke of as having "made the trip." As Rose took leave of us and faded into the mystery of Alzheimer's, I sought out Jim Burns for guidance. Only years later, as I sat next to him, did I feel I was in the presence of one who rested in the solidity of enlightenment. For woven within his outbursts of profanity, were the insights of a man who had ferociously studied his self and transcended it.

As a diagnosed schizophrenic, Jim Burns is a man tortured by his outer self for much of his life, yet truly "at home with the inner self." His illness gives him unique insight into psychology and the impetus to study the mind as, truly, his life depended on it. Perhaps his greatest gift is leaving clues for other seekers looking for inner truth. "My answer," he says, "is to know the Self."

The following book is the third edition of *At Home with the Inner Self*. The bulk of the book consists of transcripts from informal talks recorded in 1984 and 1985. New to the third edition is an interview conducted in 2006 as well as the photographs that evoke the graceful dissolution of the urban landscape that Jim calls home.

*I learned to lock onto my inner self at all times.*
~ *Jim Burns*

# Introduction

Perhaps it is best said at the outset that we consider ourselves to be at the earliest beginnings of man's first true awakening. We consider the problems of the world to be rooted in the fact that each individual person has not yet discovered the nature of his own consciousness. The grand awakening, should it ever come, would be one in which every individual person is brought to realization and complete, clear awareness of their own internal workings. We consider that in some point in time this will be required by school and statute. The general maelstrom mankind finds itself in—and has to do something to get out of—is the result of all the machinations of projection and transference in which everybody is working their own internal conflicts out on everybody else.

Freud and Jung were the godheads of a new beginning. They pointed a course as to what has to be done to get beyond the mass externalization of stress that results in bloodshed and insane, abusive wealth. Internal disharmony can be traced to being at the root of our problems from starvation to ghetto muggings, and until people are able to be responsible to themselves for themselves, there isn't a faint ray of hope. Until something is done about the source of the carnage, there is no hope on earth. Working on your own mind-set and improving your understanding of yourself and others has been alluded to since Grecian times, but it is no longer a pleasure for the idle rich, it is a necessity for every person on earth.

Everyone goes through life picking up from everybody around them pieces of mind-set that are devoted to one's own destruction. That is why you have to get down to the raw elements of where the whole thing started and trace it all the way through. I've spent forty years doing this and believe such a process is the only hope for humanity and a new dawn coming over the earth. In the destroyed condition I've been in and came back from several times in my life, I've seen what is possible and know that there is real hope. There is a process going on—we are only at the beginning.

People talk about meditation, T.M., tantra, prayer, books on philosophy and psychology, discussion groups, this and that and the other thing—but no one makes a clear statement of what they are trying to do. A person is bound to get confused. If you've gotten to a point where you realize that the thing you would like most to find in this world is a steady source of guidance, to help you become your own source of guidance—then that's what you are after. You never find that stated anywhere in simple language.

The key to the whole process lies in the fact that there is a fountain-spring of endless guidance and information within every human being. One only has to learn to get out of its way, to let the consciousness generate in a stilled and quiet mind. Because of our western heritage, I'm tempted to use the term that is common in the A.R.E. and the churches—that the Christ-head reigns supreme within. When you begin to have experiences of the information from within, you learn how perfectly attuned the inner mind is to your immediate and momentary circumstances. It can guide you exactly to the thinking required to deal with the outer circumstances or other aspects of consciousness that are absorbing your attention. It is perfectly attuned to the potential of expanding your total consciousness to its absolute maximum. It is designed to do this. It is endlessly trying to do this. It can't stop doing it. The fountainhead lies totally within. All we discuss here pertains to the methods and particulars that are involved in uncovering the wellhead.

~ James J. Burns III

# The Success Mode

I really can't talk to people who can only think about what they can get out of it. There are people who think every second they're with someone, "What's it going to get for me?" When I lived in the Squirrel Hill area of Pittsburgh, there were people there with almost exclusively that mind state. As far as I am concerned, they are a cancer.

The key to understanding the essence of the circumstances of these driven types of people, lies in the fact that they almost universally had bad childhoods, in varying degrees. It is beyond my capability to imagine a person with that unusual amount of energy to have found that energy through anything but frustration. What they are doing every day is going out the door to prove what a "good kid" they are. They don't care a thing who they kill in the process. They are still being a "good kid."

If I go out the door in the morning to be engaged with society, which is a specific feeling, for me the greatest kick is just to be knocking around with other people. It doesn't matter if it is teaching or digging ditches. This isn't true of the success-oriented person. The success-oriented person sees everything in the form of hierarchies, and evaluates everything in terms of his position on the pole, and what it's going to get him.

Nothing succeeds like success except for one thing that's wrong with it: it's addictive. Like all addictions, it takes a little more every day to get the same high. If the person is fortunate and happens to be at the right place at the right time often enough, and is also able to do what is required of him in his work without messing up wholesale in his handling of people, then he can make it and continue succeeding. In the long view, though, how many corporate presidents are there?

Obviously, the success-oriented person is necessary for our economy. But as soon as these people get into middle management positions and climb about as high as they will, their dreams begin to die. I've seen half a dozen of my friends in their fifties go through this process. Every one of them became a total loss. They start getting their hopes up about being able to accept defeat, which they are never able to completely do, and somehow crawl across the line to sixty-five and retirement, which becomes a Valhalla of sorts, whereupon they promptly die within six to eighteen months.

No matter who you are, if you don't die young, the bullshit is going to stop being bought sooner or later. If you have to prove yourself every day all over again, it gets very tiring. Even if a person doesn't know what's going on, it still gets tiring. You get all sorts of variation of reaction. One guy will go home and whimper to his wife all night, which is a common reaction. Some go whimper to the bartender. Some go whimper to their buddy. I'm referring to people who are in relatively high achievement positions. I would love to see just one case of a person who isn't like this, because I don't think there are any. I'm saying that they are poor Johnny one-notes. Some are just the opposite. They scream from the minute they come in the door until the minute they leave. If you are saddled with having to prove yourself all the time, it's a hopeless task. I thought a couple of my friends weren't going to have this problem. They got to forty-five or fifty, though, and every one of them fell apart. There has to be some who don't fall into this pattern, but I've never met them.

Although I gave up on altruism as an explanation for people's actions, there are a few people whose basic interest is knowing how to be important to other people in positive ways. They are not masochists or sadists, but a third type. These people are interested in getting the day's affairs in order and accomplished and in developing a smooth flow of effort, and so are the best kind of managers. Unfortunately there aren't too many of them.

The majority of people are motivated by their effectiveness at what they're doing. All people are effective at least to a degree at what they do. If they lose this effectiveness—although it doesn't happen too often—they just fall apart. The minute they don't have something to give them a sense of accomplishment, they have nothing to fall back on and their whole world comes apart.

The average guy has a job because the boss has to have somebody there to do it. If the boss could do it himself, the guy wouldn't be there. He doesn't see the boss that often, but generally speaking, bosses have a tendency to be a pain in the rear because of some specific reasons. The boss got to be boss because he was effective at doing something real. Now he's got nothing to do, so he has to stick his nose in somewhere it doesn't belong so he can have a feeling of effectiveness. This is the biggest problem with management. They have a tendency not to have anything real to do. It depends on the situation. Most are up to their eyes in paperwork. The paperwork isn't like being on the line and doing the work. You don't get the same sense of effectiveness out of it.

In psychological patterns, it is a matter of having or not a sense of effectiveness. If there is no one around to listen to the boss's ideas, then no matter where he is in management, in his own eyes he considers himself a peon. He's always looking to be upstairs, so he always has the inferior feeling. Every time he gets a rebuff of any kind, it comes back down the line. That's the difference between good and bad managers. The whole error in their thinking lies in that they see their whole world as tied up in their job situation. They have no world-view.

If I had had my mind and had gone into something, I would have, I think, come to the place where I was doing as much as I wanted to do. I've known a few people who consistently turned down promotions because they didn't want to be bothered with the pressure of the higher level. The trouble with most corporations is that they won't let you get away with it. You turn down a promotion and they end up firing you.

To me, the idea was to run just as fast as the situation pulled me. I wasn't interested in being anything beyond what I wanted to be. I knew that in myself I didn't want to be over-driven. I knew too many people who were in way over their heads.

In the matter of continuing to maintain a sense of function and capability, which is the key to the whole thing, there are people who want to feel personally close to those around them, and there are people who abhor it. The ones who abhor it are the ones who have the negative pattern of having never known what it was like to be cooperative with anyone in their life.

When I was working and had any type of job with people working for me, the thing that was most important to me was the sense of personal involvement. There are some people you work with who don't want any part of it. They can't tolerate the sense of closeness, any kind of a sign of closeness. They want to come in, do their work and leave, and they have nothing to do with you personally. There are others who are just crazy to have company.

We are always looking for an expansion of the communal feeling. The fact that people do this or that because there is a buck in it is what kills it. It is cheap prostitution. The power-chaser will never let you see his soft side. On the other hand, a person who tries to be all heart with people will never let you see how they cheated someone. Generally, neither can even see it themselves. That place in the middle is what we're seeking. The more good company you are, the more you get. The more you give, the more you get.

"Positive thinking" or "correct mental attitude" has nothing to do with success. If you examine the people who propose these theories and say that they are responsible for their success, you find the theory has nothing to do with it. They were in the place where it happened, and there's nothing more to it. It is outside our range of control. Success comes to one person and not another, and there's no accounting for it. There is no rich man who ever created a family of rich men. There is no king who ever created a king. There is no philosopher who ever created a philosopher. It just doesn't work that way. Our type of comprehension wants us to believe that when we get smart enough we'll achieve success. This is the tragedy of the ego.

At puberty and after puberty, for a certain period of time, there's a possibility of knowing that what you want to know is about your own internal nature. If you don't have any reinforcement to know what you can find, you don't find anything that means anything to you. So you end up losing the opportunity. Once you lose the opportunity, the urge gets misplaced or sublimated into the urge for material things, status, and all the rest of it. But you can never satisfy the need for a square peg with a round one. You can just never do it. You can chase it all your life and never get any measure of what you are looking for.

What is unhappiness? People are unhappy and never question it. If what you have now makes you unhappy, what would make you happy? In each person's mind are a certain number of routes to his own fulfillment. They are different from person to person. What are you really striving for? It is the desire for a fulfillment that can't be found in the marketplace.

I am convinced that the people who succeed in this world in the ordinary sense, have views of the world that permit them to maintain fantasies that will not suffer examination. Their head is addicted to some view that permits their mind to function in a response pattern where they are beyond the capacity of doubting. This is not really bad. There would be no life on earth as we know it if it weren't so. We have the belief that we have to answer to success in order to answer to our own inner needs. It is a fallacy of reasoning that is almost universal. We're putting round pegs in square holes. It is an inaccurate view of what our needs truly are.

I have had a very clear outer mind at times in my life. This permitted me to understand that when a mind is free of the inner stress, it hungers for activity in the outer world. Not for the purpose of success, but for the purpose of utilization of energy, to maintain a sense of internal tranquility. As soon as you're doing something in terms of success, you're off the track. The reason you do things is that the pressure is there to do so. If you do nothing, the build-up becomes unbearable. The doing is the satisfaction, not the successfulness. The real relief is finding a place to put the energy that answers to itself in the doing of it.

The other day I was coming from downtown Pittsburgh on the bus. There was a street person who got on the bus. You don't see nearly as many of these people in Pittsburgh as you do in some of the bigger cities. This person was probably in her fifties, massively overweight, wearing about five coats, the last of which just fit around her and was buttoned at the top. She had on a knit hat and was carrying four cloth shopping bags. Because of my knowledge of these people, I knew she was carrying everything she owned. She was completely out of her shoes—her feet were sticking out all over. And because it was cold, she had on about three pairs of stockings and then a pair of socks. It's a great question whether she had a regular place to sleep.

Now this can be very upsetting. It is upsetting to everyone on that bus, whether they know it or not. We all identify with the possibility of being in that condition, even if we don't realize it. It's automatic. This is why we like to be near successful people. The load is less. That's the only reason. The mutual responsibility is less, period. But if you get too far down the road, being around successful people can be a very bad drain because that side of your being feels inferior. You find yourself in the flip-flop of the thing.

I lived in the YMCA downtown and all the rest of it. It's an existence that completely eschews the success mode. For one reason, it isn't available to these people. Anyone, on the other hand, who answers to the success mode in that their bills are regularly paid and they can be looked upon as being about the norm in society... So long as these conditions are met, a person is incapable of escaping it. It requires personal failure to generate insight, the way we go about it.

It is my hope that when we come to know how to answer to the inner being as its capacity develops in children—if we come upon that line and never lose it, we can attain the ability for insight by a totally painless route. The way it is now, it takes a crash before the outer self can be forced to admit that there even is an inner self.

# Society

By design, everybody from the beginning of mankind until now starts with the notion that life is a bed of roses, it's nothing but kicks, a glory road. That's the way your mind points when you are born. Our mind is of such a nature that it cannot survive and won't work without a fantasy, a fantasy that has nothing to do with reality. If you get stuck looking at too much reality, you're going to come apart at the seams. Life will become meaningless and your mind will refuse to have anything to do with it. The longer you live—if you live long enough and can maintain any essence of sanity—you discover that these fantasies are built into your head to keep you putting up with it. You may get to the point where you're not willing to put up with it under any circumstances, and your mind collapses, which is what happened to me.

The whole of society is endlessly trying to make good on things that are worthless. They spend their lifetime pumping themselves up with fantasy because they can't stand the facts. By design you are extremely limited from this physical side as to what you're supposed to be concerned with. You cannot maintain interest in what you're not designed to be playing with. Although we're designed to look at the world a certain way, when you start calling this basic design "Pollyanna," you are in trouble over your eyeballs.

Anything that pays the bills or works in the everyday world, including psychological systems, is never able to be rejected or seen for its errors. As long as you pay the bills, you have little chance of escaping your thought patterns. You never get to see how things are on the other side of the street, so to speak. If it works, it is self-maintaining, including all the mistakes built into the mind-set.

The average person has a set of succeeding habits designed to master the simple production of livelihood and never seriously questions life unless he has a disastrous defeat. You are incapable of it. Knowing this is necessary in order to understand people's personal psychologies. You never get to the other side of the street because you are satisfied with what is on your side. This is why the older a person gets, the narrower their inner options get. They've been successful for so long in looking at things one way. We're creatures of habit. We want to have all the answers out in front of us and everything ready. That's why a person always goes back to his old answers. You're in a dilemma. You do want to change, but you don't want to change. It's threatening and painful to change. The essence of change is discomfort. People only go as far as they need to go.

There are very few people who have the capacity to separate themselves from the people around them. Familiarity breeds contempt. You don't knowingly heap yourself with your own abuse, you heap somebody else with it. This is all to answer the need for getting the crops in. When you are threatened, you "dump" it on everyone and anyone who is available in order to get free enough to be able to do the day's work. You've got to get free enough to be able to accomplish a day's work, pay the bills, and get fed. It all comes back to that first necessity of survival that we're all painfully grinding on. All of us.

The average person—due to the needs of the functions of projection and transference—is out working on somebody else all the time without knowing they are doing it, trying to discharge their own anxieties. Some actually live on other people's pain. It's what keeps them going and how they get their feeling of effectiveness. Their unconscious reactions come out as sadism, which gives the person enough of a day-to-day high to keep on going. Transference, projection, and the like obviously work, because they keep people out of the booby hatch.

People keep to themselves because of the threat of being blown out of their own mental cocoon. People who can't stand to have other people in their home or go out in public are on such a tight little island because they are sitting on the killing urge. They feel so terribly threatened that they have to go to all of these extremes to keep from killing something. They *have* to walk in a tight little circle.

You may not be as fragile when you get out of childhood and adolescence, but no one is autonomous. Can you actually say you can get by without any good experience? You never get autonomous from your family. Your family extends into your peer group. And you die dealing with your family and peer group. The only thing you have to take into the foray is the mind-set that was cast upon you as a child, and *that* you cannot change.

If you like a person, you are inclined to show it to them. While some people avoid others, some see their solutions in others. With the security-seeking type of person, you are always being tested. They are incapable of a level relationship with somebody. They can only be inferior or superior. It is because of their desire to work out of the environment the factor they need to feel secure. But, so long as you are seeking security, you cannot achieve it. This is a broad-based characteristic in many people and, oddly, nearly has become the basis of our society.

You are in a social circumstance so long as you still remember your last face-to-face confrontation or are under the influence of it. Your entire being is affected. This applies whether the confrontation was verbal or nonverbal. The point is that you have to become aware that so long as you are within eyeshot or earshot, you are constantly being affected by the internal condition of those around you. If they have no idea of their internal turmoil, then it is left for you to deal with, which is how most people get along.

If the average person's mind was hooked to a loudspeaker and you could hear what went through it, you would probably look for the highest building around so you could be dead the first time. You are walking around in a reality that is the production of this common consciousness. There are very few who understand the functions that the mind is trying to fulfill and maintain. My view of the common consciousness is that it is a trash heap, a moldering dung heap. How many people do you know who are clearly conscious of—and broadly and deeply versed in—the information required to insure that their children will have insight, understanding, and wisdom?

Normal people would do anything on earth to avoid talking about or looking at what goes on in their own head. That thought led me to the first clear insight I ever had: "These people are crazy!" I was just a kid. Then I spent a year on who was crazy. They were out there living in the world, and I was just a kid. They paid the bills but were scared to death of their own heads. So I was crazy, but who was sane? Something that helped me was the thought that I was crazy, but that it was a perfectly normal reaction to the circumstance. That left me off a big hook. People defend themselves from their own best interests, and don't know to stop it. The objective is to find a natural process to come back into operation. It comes back in spontaneously. You stumble onto it, then you learn how to use it. The thing is that you have an ego set up, without knowing how it came into existence or the ramifications of it, that prevents you. It has to leak through, or trick you out of the way, so to speak, so you can get out there where you can see things.

In this world there are two available mind-sets. One direction is to experience Truth, to know what it means to light your whole body up with insight, to make it your highest goal, to have the experience of overwhelming insight and comprehension of the whole realm of human experience. That's one mind-set or direction that accounts for maybe one hundredth of one percent of the total. The entire rest of the mind-sets is what you are involved in in everyday life, and is running away from the first mind-set. You are terrified by it. Everything everybody does is designed to destroy the possibility of ever getting to the first mind-set. That is the big problem.

The average person's mind is full of so much tripe and garbage, and is so far divorced from understanding what is going on here, that the miracle is that anything gets accomplished. If it weren't for mankind's capability of reducing complex tasks into simple repetitive tasks, we'd have nothing. If it required a creative imagination every minute to survive, the survival rate would be zero. The average mind is a garbage heap that is ninety-nine percent disabled.

My view is that through our capacity to reduce things to simple elements, and resultantly the ability to maintain vast hordes of people in a very materially comfortable life through simple efforts, that we've finally gotten to the point where we've bought enough time for a few people who have the genetic propensity, to be the resolvers, the true researchers, the perceivers of new information and insight into the workings of the mind. We finally have the circumstances where they can maintain themselves while trying to do this work.

If we survive without a nuclear war—which I don't think we will—but if we should happen to, and get another 300 years or so of working on consciousness, we will have in fact the Garden of Eden. If we could train people to have the capacity to come to their own fulfillment in minding their own business instead of somebody else's business, we would have such a blissful state on earth that it truly would be the Garden of Eden. That's my view of what could be.

# "Mental Illness"

You have to have some form of work. I could say universally that all the long-term patients I knew in mental institutions were there largely because, for some reason or another, they missed the time to plug themselves into the work-a-day world, to find their place. Most were browbeaten so badly by their surroundings that they never had a chance to get up off the floor. If this goes on long enough, it becomes a habit pattern. They learn to dodge themselves and the things around them by going internally. Not in the sense of insight, but in the sense of withdrawal. They go into a state you and I would call "numbness." When something traumatic occurs, you can go numb in reaction to it. It is like when a fuse blows. It's too much to handle. You have to back up and take it a piece at a time. If things are too overwhelming, you go numb. If you can't stand the numbness, you go into a rage.

What they do is that their mind recycles on very short patterns, at least in some. They think about very little things in circles. The thing it effectively does is keep their attention span down to zero. If the attention span is kept down, you never have enough clearness to be aware of the pain. The mind does this as a protective mechanism. When somebody is forced into this pattern just after puberty—which is when all hell breaks loose—for any period of time over a year, then there is no changing it during their lifetime. It

*E.D.*

can't be done. I am lucky to have had the strange set of experiences that permitted me to become insightful instead of "circular." This type of circular thinker is a very small percentage of the population even in institutions.

"Defenses" aren't actually defenses, they're offences. Your defenses are you resisting the idea that you are sick. When you go through the full-blown emotional experience of realizing that you are sick, guess what will happen? You will fight the thing right down to a stop, a death, an ego death. When it's over, you will no longer be sick. Sickness is about the emotional response to the realization of sickness. What is unusual about me is that I went through ego death when I was thirteen, and that was why I could study madness. The way out is through the middle, the only way out. I've been crazy, and I know everything there is to know about it. The craziest are those who are running away from it.

Every time you deal with a deflated ego, you always find that the child part of you is behind it. Roughly speaking, the way it goes is... You may be driving down the road and you're thinking... I assume you accept the fact that you discover what you are thinking and darn near never decide what you're thinking, which is the fix we are all stuck with. You notice you're bent out of shape about something, but can't quite put your finger on what it is. You might be thinking about why you're driving an old junker instead of a new Cavalier, and on, and on.

You have to start by identifying what is causing the problem in the clearest concepts possible, and let your thoughts run before you can find what is behind them. All of anxiety, shame, guilt, and fear are generally wrapped up in the area of self-rejection. When some part of you is pounding at you, it's because it isn't getting something. When you can learn how to give it what it needs, it shuts up, whether it is the "child," the "adult," or the "engineer" moderator part of you between the two. This is three different people. The key to the whole thing is tied in the hope that if you can find out what that part of you is really after, you can put it to rest.

When you get into childish blind emotions, you have to go into them and find out what is behind them. When, on the other hand, it is the ego that is agitated, it's because you have not let the process of imagining run far enough ahead. In other words, the ego part of comprehension operates on the basis of images of where you want to go. When your ego starts hammering you, it's because you're not paying attention to what it is trying to give you as input in the process of letting your imagination run far enough to say that "this is what you want." It wants you to reach for this. It's hammering you because it's not getting its point across.

The more effective you become at being the "engineer," the more that's the person you become. That's the identity you develop. The engineer becomes the central ego. You're in the process of becoming one person out of the three that would never have been there without the effort. You become an entirely different person. Eventually this third self becomes the only person that remains. The other two selves just become aspects of the central engineer.

The way it starts with everyone is that they stumble into the bad side of internal experience. You never stumble into the good side of internal experience. Nobody does. I never heard of a case. It always starts out with the nightmares getting you, and that forces you to do something about it. After years of sweating blood, you get to the point where you start working your way out of the mire. Then comes the good time, but only later. In the last analysis, some variation of inner sickness is the human condition for the reason that we have not yet learned enough to not have it be so. The paradise mankind is looking for lies in the direction of knowing enough about the psyche to raise children so that they never have to be sick. Children have to be raised to have an inner life.

People will die before they admit that they have an inner problem. So long as any part of you is strongly denying a problem, you can see why they say schizophrenia—two persons. One of you knows as well as it knows anything that something is seriously wrong. The other part of you is saying "I am never going to cast myself with the outcasts." It's two egos fighting.

One ego says you're sick, that something is wrong. The other claims it's not true. You can never let go of the ego that knows something is wrong. You can never achieve it. You can let go of the one, but you can't let go of the other. If you want to bleed it down, just let the words "I'm a freak, a mental case" play over and over in your mind. All the aberrations come in when the energies of the two egos—the one that says you're OK and the one that says you're not—collide.

All mental illness is the result of loneliness. Freud makes the remark somewhere that mental illness exhibits itself when the person first experiences the depths of loneliness. This is true no matter what the age. That's when it starts. If you are true to yourself, you will be abandoned, and you will do anything to avoid abandonment— which is the whole crux of the internal argument. The reason I got so violently sick when I was young was because I realized how wrong everybody's life was. If I'd have been able to go along with all their B.S., I'd have never been sick.

We are gregarious by nature, and the minute we start to feel separated, we are in trouble. This is because of the habit built into us of blaming ourselves instead of others. Seeing through this habit was the big difference for me. When I was driven crazy, I knew it was others who did it. I fought with the instinct to blame myself and said to myself that I wouldn't buy it, that they caused the condition and not me, that they were responsible and not me. That was why I was such an oddball among the mentally ill. The mentally ill go around all day smearing feces on their face and the like, and doing everything they can that is self-demeaning. Their behavior is symbolic. In one form or another they are saying to the world, "Look what you did to me!" But they do not go through the consciousness of it. Everything they do speaks to the issue of "Look what you've done to me." It is easier for them to blame themselves than to face the abyss of isolation.

When two people have an argument, it is similar to what occurs when two parts of the self are arguing. When two people come to a resolution, how is it possible? There is something in it for both sides. That's the only way resolution is possible. People argue about the fact that they want "theirs" every time.

In an argument, one side says something and the other comes in and modifies it. This process goes on until the two become clear about what they want. Afterwards, they don't know what the argument was about, because if they had looked, the answer was there from the beginning. Until the people look across the street and see what they want, the argument will go on.

With psychological problems, the only way that the part of you that says you're sick can win the argument is if it can make it blatantly obvious. The more you resist, the crazier you get is how the pattern works, until you break down and say to yourself, "All right! All right! I'm crazy as a loon!" The other side collapses under the load. The part of you that wants to demonstrate how crazy you are is the emotional side, which people instinctively feel is right on the dark edge of the abyss. The part of you that wants to demonstrate that there is really nothing seriously wrong is the mental side. When the emotional side has spent itself through the admission that you really are crazy, then the mental side has calm to deal with.

The inner argument goes on and on and chops away, a little at a time, showing you how sick you are. It's saying, "Look how sick you are, you idiot! When are you going to get wise!" It's serving a legitimate function. It's making it unavoidably clear that there's something wrong. When it's finally made the whole point as an emotional experience, it just goes phhhttt. It's gone. Your mind doesn't set up all that energy for no reason. It's trying to do you a favor, but you will shake the shake of the damned before you can let go. But at the other end is the golden field.

When the emotional part has peaked, when it has driven you in your own experience in consciousness to the point where you realize you are completely bananas, then the ego dies. That's the emotional side's function. Then you say, "Ahh, yes...," and the whole thing is over. You are no longer the same person. You no longer live in the same reality. It will take awhile before you realize some of the differences. You no longer strive to be like the people you have been unknowingly striving to be like. You look at people and realize that every one of them is wacky. It's an entirely different reality. The argument is gone. Both sides die and you become a new third person. You are back to spontaneity versus constantly planning. You are back to where you started with the exception of knowing how you got there.

What finally happens is that you realize everyone is messed up, so what the heck. But only after it has driven you through the agony of response and ego death. You say to yourself: "Every ounce of my energy, every second of my consciousness, is caught up in this %$&#$! thing. I just can't stand it anymore!" It'll work you until you drop.

When it occurs to you that you have psychological problems, the first reaction that happens is "What did I do wrong?" That's why your ego fights it for so long, because you paint it on yourself. You blame it on yourself, and you go through a whole round robin until you come to the point where you say, "Wait a minute here, Jack. Where's the baby that can change its own diaper? Where's the infant that can form its own mind? Somebody messed me over." Before you know anything about how they did it, know that they did it.

The question is not really whether you did something wrong, but did you learn something? That's all. The worst parental attitude is the same as that of the Catholic Church, that you are *ipso facto* wrong, that there is nothing right about you, and that you couldn't do anything right except occasionally by accident. The business of your mind getting going on that "something is wrong" can be a blind alley. I'm not saying it always is.

You cannot do anything, this side of total insanity, that comes to you as being a wrong action that is not some form of hostility. You cannot have a hostile reaction without a cause. The cause is always not being understood when you wanted to be. It is not having the opportunity to talk to someone about what was on your mind, and be understood. When you talk about cause-and-effect chains, I will make the claim that there can never be anything that comes to guilt that did not start as loneliness. As a result I quit dealing with guilt altogether. I went back to the loneliness and dealt with that, and the guilt just doesn't exist. It evaporates. Guilt is one of those traps. Loneliness is something that always afflicts those with high IQs. They have nobody who takes as obvious the things they take as obvious. They are bound into higher concepts.

If you are into working on consciousness, into seeking to unlock the hidden resources, you aren't going to find much company. Let's hope you find enough company. The average person is so frightened of these things that if he ever gets an insight into them, he will run away and never come back. I really think it takes a conscious effort to stay away from inner study. Instinctively people know that they have the same problems and questions, but a little less of it. They can play the game of "stay away," and they stay away as long as they can, just the same as you or I did. "Why" is because it is more important to get your face fixed than to get your head fixed. There's nothing more difficult than this work, but if you want to know what it's like to feel like a giant, wait until you get to the other side of this mountain.

I never saw anyone who didn't take this inner conflict down to the last agonizing grunt. Until you are prostrate and totally without energy to fight it, you can't let it overcome you. And until you can let it overcome you, you can't be set free. To have any choice about the matter is almost impossible. If you have the opportunity to let it loose, don't deny yourself the opportunity.

If something is serious enough that it keeps coming to the surface, sooner or later it will come to the point of you using all your energy to try to keep away from it. My doctor used to be the automobile. I drove hundreds of thousands of miles. It gives the outer mind just enough to do that it allows the inner mind to come up for some air. Whatever is trying to get to the surface, don't be startled by its first form. What it really is, is likely an eternity away from what you think it is. I never saw anyone who wasn't brought to a crossroads before they achieved insight. I just wish I knew why it is this way. Until you are total wreckage you can't get saved. That upsets me.

The first thing that comes to your mind when you finally have to let go, is that it is the end of your world. You think your mind is going to run amuck and they're going to find you running down the middle of the street babbling at the moon. The first time it happened to me I only ended laying down face first in my room for about twenty minutes. It was the rage to live. To be alive, to know, to feel, to love, to be.

# Method

We were talking about free association, the other night after someone brought up the point. This point needs to be brought up. When I was doing this, I had no one to talk to. I had no one to turn to. I had no place to go to discuss things. So apparently, the forces that exist decided that they were going to give me the special gift of teaching me how to do my own learning, how to do my own teaching, how to do my own insighting. I learned how to free associate. I asked myself the questions that would take me out of the blind spots. Most people doing this get into a blind spot, get into a thought that becomes repetitive, and they're done. You don't know where to go with it.

People get into a blind spot and might stay there for the rest of their life. I didn't have that problem. I learned to ask myself the questions: What does it look like? What does it feel like? What does it seem like? What does it act like? Endlessly asking myself questions. Until suddenly there was one thought that was blank and would go no further. The free association word wouldn't yield anything like the release necessary. I would change just one little inflection in the words as I repeated them in my mind, just one little inflection. I'd ask myself: What does this mean? What does it suggest? What does that make me think of? I never found one of them that I didn't find my way out of, whatever trap

I got into by doing that. I don't know anybody else who knows how to guide themselves out of that hole. I can guide someone else out of a hole, but I can't seem to teach them how to do it themselves.

Everything you've gone through in your lifetime and haven't resolved is still sitting there waiting to be worked on. Either you get straight with some of this stuff, or you'll wish you had. It is a mountain of work. You don't deal with each individual circumstance but with the abstraction of the problem. You deal with the still-existing patterns. You don't deal with the individual circumstances of things in your life. The singular psychological patterns that maintain presently-held values and patterns of thinking are what you deal with. You don't deal with the individual circumstances that gradually imbued you with one particular aspect or complex. Even then it is a mountain of work.

The ability of getting a feeling to translate into words is a tricky business, but it is well worth the effort. When some insight comes up, you should stop everything you are doing, if at all possible, and pay attention to it. If a word associated with a current feeling comes up, it is often extremely important. Repeat the word until you get some sense of what it means. It is often a word at the crossroads of other concepts, and ties them together. Before you couldn't figure out how this tied into this or this tied into that. You begin to build a structure and develop comprehension.

If you hold center on a problem long enough, things will open up. It is difficult when you are first trying this. It takes a while to develop the expertise. Sometimes the effort of trying to hold center and bring something up is so great that you simply can't do it. It takes practice. You're facing a void because you don't know what you're looking for. If you keep mentally facing forward, it will eventually focus itself. You'll focus what your inner nature is seeking. If there wasn't an unanswered and even misstated question, you wouldn't be doing this. At this point the question isn't even formed. You just know that there has to be a better state than that which you are currently in. The unanswered is what you are seeking.

It is difficult to stay on the point when thinking about something. It may be something so painful to you that the mind will keep drifting to almost anything to get off the painful thought. When facing the unknown, the key is overcoming the fear. You must have faith that it will work. Fear is absolutely the hallmark that you are getting near something important. When you get to this fear, you know something you are looking for will be found. You know that you've found a hot spot.

You have to have consistency in doing this and facing it to produce results. You can't meditate this week, do it again next week, and then let it go. You'll wind up always going back to the beginning. On the other hand, don't expect too much of yourself. When it gets too hot, let it go for awhile. The next time around, you'll be a little closer when you start, and you'll go a little farther before becoming uncomfortable again.

If you're being bothered by something, I've found that if you let your body run the show, just lying horizontal, that all the things that wander around in your mind will drift off. You'll start getting a feeling that an important thought is coming. It's a physical feeling that a thought is coming up into your brain. As soon as this happens, you know you're on the road home. The pain diminishes and you start realizing what is disturbing you.

Learning this technique is like learning a new language. The first couple of times it is not going to be very effective. You just have to lie there and be quiet until the problem comes to the surface. You have to face forward into the void, as it were, a type of tunnel vision. Ideas will come to you, and eventually one will come that really hits the gong about problems you are facing. Different ideas will come to fill that void. The thing that is hard about it, when you're first attempting it, is to realize that you're searching for something you presently have no answer to. It is hard to realize that you are putting effort into something where there is now nothing, as far as consciousness is concerned. I came upon this method instinctively. For the first year I wondered what the heck I was trying to do. Finally it started to work. This meditation—and dreams—is where I've learned everything. And I never learned anything from a book.

You may unconsciously be chastising yourself that inner work is not a good use of time and energy. You may be prejudiced against your own thinking to what someone else says or what you read in a book. You have to think as much of your own thoughts as you do of somebody else's. In any effort you start out from zero. You may feel foolish about the things you are thinking about but you have to start somewhere. You have to realize that you are trying to be a student of yourself and that it is a good effort.

I was stumbling around with meditation, and I discovered that if something was bothering me and an answer to the problem occurred to me, then it stopped bothering me. So when something started bothering me, I knew I was looking for a specific answer, which was the golden key to the thing. Little did I realize how much work it would be. At first you don't know what you are seeking. Once you make the discovery of this inner satisfaction, then you know what you are seeking. You're blind to it for quite awhile. You just know things aren't what you'd like, but you aren't able to be specific about it.

Our major appetite is the need to comprehend. Comprehension is a specific appetite and even needs to understand itself. You need to know what the mind is trying to get done so you can be more effective at it. Your internal system is entirely capable, given the opportunity, of teaching you what it is trying to teach you. Your inner being knows. Your outer being is always unknowing. Your system is constantly trying to get some inner job done. It is constantly trying to get you to be conscious of what is distressing you. Secondly, it is trying to get you to comprehend the natural laws and patterns in which that particular distress is involved. To know where the mistake is so you can avoid making the mistake and start going with the natural flow. This is all built in by design.

Try to place the problem mentally in front of you and let every tension go out of your body. Let the thing just hang in front of you. Gradually, a word will come to mind that will begin to explain and alleviate the circumstances. The words form so long as you hold that center. It is uncomfortable and miserable, and the only thing that is worse is that which you're trying to escape. If it is something superficial, you can deal with it superficially. If it is a deeper problem, you have to pinpoint what is bothering you. To find out what it is, you have to stay on center on the problem and not slip off the point. Sometimes a flash of insight might come, which lasts but milliseconds. If you miss it, you can only get back to that insight by plodding and working step by step.

You can bring on insight experiences if you learn how. You have to let go of the trivia. But you have to learn what the trivia is in reference to what you're seeking. It may not be trivia in all situations. Some insight might come up when you're at a business meeting. Now to me, for the time being, the meeting would be trivial because it is merely readily accessible, and I'd have to get away—maybe excusing myself to go to the bathroom—to get at the source of what's coming up. You may have to try to get a handle on it by repeating the word or concept over and over to yourself. When you get a handle on it, you can remember it to get back to later. If you let it go, it may not come again. It is a way of life. You don't want to give your job away, but you have to do whatever is possible.

When you run the gamut of concentrating on something, you may want to take a break or forget it for awhile. Just when you take your mind off it, is when answers to your other problems will often come into view. This is a good thing to know from the methodological standpoint. The reason for it is very simple: when you are keyed up and putting a lot of energy into a problem, the minute you let go of the problem, all the energy has to go somewhere, and it goes to whatever the next problem is on your agenda—in priority— even if you don't know consciously what your next priority problem may be. The second you break off concentration, a slight dizziness sets in because of the change in concentration levels. That is when the answers will come in. The more you do this switching back and forth of levels, the more effective this process and information is. As soon as you take this high-energy level off the problem you are focusing on, it will escape to the next energy level like a spark crossing the gap in a spark plug. Until you are good at it, you won't notice it. It will just go flashing by.

There is a free association part of the mind that is like a citizen's band scanner, constantly going up and down the channels. Your inner mind is constantly trying to get your outer self to be aware of what's going on within yourself until you've answered to that need. It keeps throwing balls over the fence. As you drive down the road your mind will constantly pick out this fence or that tree, or this sign. You're accustomed to it and assume that everyone else's mind does the same thing. If you analyzed why you pick this or that to see out of everything that is available, you'll see that there's a definite reason and pattern to it. It follows very closely the things that come in ordinary dreaming, which is another method of throwing balls over the fence. The dream-maker uses these things in waking life. They are attempts to guide you to what in you is unfulfilled.

When I was young, I learned that dreams were the source of all necessary information. It's good to go to sleep slowly and to wake up slowly. If you have a nagging dream, just lie in bed and be quiet. Try and be conscious of no-thing, which is different than nothing. Just let it come to you. All the pictography of the dream is an attempt by the inner stage master to throw things over the fence to key you in to what is happening in your insides. Through dreams, you can repair the bridge to the inner self and again become a whole person. Realizing something in a dream isn't enough—you have to become aware of it in the waking state.

When I was good at interpreting dreams, several times I was able to go deep inside myself and hear and see the dream as it was explained. I was actually able to get a person to repeat what they said time after time until I was able to re-experience the dream. In interpreting my own dreams, what I would do when I woke up was to go all the way back to the crossover state, the borderland between fully awake and fully asleep. The feelings that the dreams elicit are the things that tell you what the dream means, so you have to be able to go right back into it. Whatever the same feelings are that would occur to you when you are awake, is what the dream is trying to get to. The real point in dreams is to get it to come back so clearly that you get all the feelings as they went by.

Your inner mind is using all opportunities at all times to get you to look at something about yourself. When I had my mind and could use it, every time I found somebody I didn't like, invariably I would discover that they had something that I didn't think I could ever have. But the process of going from the initial dislike to the discovery of the secret jealousy took me months every time to work my way through it. As I'd go through the process of discovering specifically what characteristics I was so jealous about, I'd find out that the person really didn't even possess the characteristics. My mind was just using the characteristic to bait me, to bring into my awareness something about my own values: that there is something that I consider to be important inside that I'm not consciously aware of. Your mind only uses these circumstances to bring your attention to something. When the washout was over with, what I would find out about the situation was that there was something that I valued that I never realized that I valued. My mind was just using the opportunity to bring it into view. You can't know what your real attitudes are until you get good at inner work. It's the only way you can find out.

Use your mind to see the implications of everything. It is an offense against a very offensive reality. You can do something about it. The people who can't do anything about it are the 99% of the population that don't know what hit them. The minute you see you can do something about it, you cease to be one of those people, although it may take awhile before it dawns on you.

The classic idea about going to a psychiatrist is that they set you down and want to know about your past. I don't want to know anything about the past, but about what brought the person in today. It is like a person looking for their glasses, and where are they? Right on their head. If I had been an analyst, a lot of the type of material I'd have written is in D.W. Winnicott's book, *The Maturational Process*. You couldn't spend enough time on it.

You don't have to remember anything, traumas and the like. You are never dealing with anything except what is right here. How long it has been there is yet another aspect. The Freudian notion that you can go into your past and set yourself free is totally false. They only achieve remembering things. That has nothing to do with it. You have to deal with the weird things you are doing now, that you started doing back then. You don't have to remember anything.

When you find the deepest past as the real now... In other words, when you find that deep past, the real now will never be the same again. When you realize that something you started nearly from the moment you were born is something you are doing right now, it instantaneously changes within you and will never be the same again. You don't go back. You go along the surface until you find the past in it. You don't go anywhere. It's all right here. It never really went anyplace. It's still here.

"The Truth will set you free." There are times you are set free and you don't even know what the truth was that did it. You have to search for the concept that expresses it. It is important to search for the concept. When you find the concept that sets you free from something, and you understand how it explains a natural process that was aborted and then brought back on track, you experience a shift of realities that will take you away from the mundane for all time, the first time it happens. It can happen in a repetitive stream for half a lifetime. You are never again caught in the surface of things. You can withdraw from the surface of things and see the overriding influence that causes situations. The first time you escape the surface of things, you are relieved of it and never caught or bound in it again.

Nobody knows this when they are studying themselves. They stumble along and fall into it and get set loose from the whole thing. Sometimes they think they've lost all their sense of reality, because reality is never perceived again as the same thing from that time on. Reality is a matter of concepts. The usual meaning of choice, the usual meaning of will, the usual meaning of self-determination are linguistic concepts that are darn near necessary. Up until this point, the most real thing in life is a hammer. After you've crossed this invisible line, the concept of "hammer" is much more real than the hammer itself. Without the concept, you couldn't have the hammer, but up until this point you couldn't appreciate the importance of that thought.

I accept the unfoldment of me before the only audience that matters — me. I long ago came to the realization that it has been completely out of my hands from the beginning. I know I've had nothing to do with what I've gone through. I've been the little character that sits at the crossroads. Nothing more, nothing less.

I have not had the opportunity that most people have had of being in the ordinary sense self-determining. They determine what they want to do, go out and do it, and have a reasonable amount of success. They pay their own bills and are able to do what they call "stand on their own feet." They have the ego support involved in it, and it becomes a large part of their view of themselves. You must remember that I have had none of this. The body is built to answer to the first necessity. Get the bills paid. Get the food on. Get the house in shape. My hunch is that the only reason I can still put up with life is because of the experiences I've had. For me to continue life would seem to make no sense.

Recently, a friend talked about the fact that he gets so despondent. He'll get a rush of insight about something, and it will trigger a flood of insights that will come. He'll be uplifted by the passing flood of insights, even about minute things but mostly the seeing into important things he's been blind to. Then he'll go to bed one night and wake up completely in a hole and not know how he got there. The insight is gone. He loses all the insights. He can't remember anything that he's gained. He feels completely dissipated and spent and doesn't know what hit him.

I really raised his eyebrows when I told him that the whole point of the conscious effort, the whole thing you want about insight, is the insight to insight. You want to be able to get to the point where you can see how to bring insight into the hole, to keep it from crushing all the progress. That's the only impediment to an endless, continual consciousness of insight, which is what I finally got to. The key was to seek and pray—literally pray—for the insight to see what causes the depressions, because the depressions are what destroy everything.

Every time you have a specific fall into a depression, one specific emotional experience is involved in it, and only one. There can be a string of depressions caused by different emotions. When you resolve and dispel one big depression through conscious effort and insight—if you ever accomplish this once—you've learned the root to dispelling all depression. Free association is the biggest key. Also, you conquer the hopelessness by facing it.

The minute you can generate a goal, depression dies. The bad thing about depression is that you can't generate a goal. A negative long-span thinking situation is always a case of the dog chasing his tail.

To be genuinely clear, which doesn't have anything to do with Scientology's "clear," is to have answered every question you have had to date, and I've been there on a regular basis. If that isn't paradise, I don't know what is. It is to have taken every feeling that ever came into your comprehension and to have traced it all the way back to its roots.

A funny thing about depression is that it takes just as much effort as it does to be positive, but you end up with totally different results. The activity itself is not so much the key as what it produces. Being positive about things is equally as real as being negative. You have the same input, different outlook and results. The only way you can determine better or not between them is by what they produce. Between them they both suffice.

If you let negativity get hold of you, it becomes consuming and you are negative about everything. There is nothing worse and more draining than having to hate. About the only way you can correct it is to be positive about little things at a time.

# Childhood

Starting as a child, you seek guidance out-side yourself because you know no better and you don't have the brain to even imagine being a source of your own guidance. Everyone wants to belong, and when you are a child you want to belong to all of the idiots who don't think, which is the whole crux of the problem. Ultimately your own system is the guidance you're seeking and is perfectly attuned to your circumstance.

In the short of it, without knowing it, a child thinks that its parents are God. Only later does the brain develop to the point where the child can have a concept of God, beyond the concept of parents. You must constantly keep this in mind when dealing with young children, because if you are harsh or strong with them, they think "God" is attacking them. They think God is all knowing, they think God's knowledge is absolute and infallible. So if God is attacking them, they must be evil. The reason you have to be careful with them is because they can fall into thinking they are evil and never know what happened.

This carries into adulthood when people throw God out the window. It is because they cannot stand the pressure of feeling worthless, useless, evil—and they have to throw away the thing that is making them feel that way. When one has the concept of an all-powerful God, and one sees people who are casting you upon yourself and making you feel inferior, guilty, worthless, useless, evil, one has to throw away the concept as worthless. You are going to try and maintain your own sense of worth. You get to the point of not being able to tolerate the thought of not seeing an end to it all. The "devil" exists because of frustration. The real black forces of this earth are the pent-up forces of frustration; the desire to be positive forced to be negative. It's a half-truth based on ignorance, and a half-truth can be more dangerous than ignorance.

We are born with fantasies. The child believes his parents are God, and they are exactly equal to the job. The first time he suffers any discomfort, he can't make any sense of it. It is in complete violation to the way his mind works. The reason they give you the idea of "God on high" is because when you were a child, you lived in a land of giants. One of the most important things you can do with your children is to get down on the floor and play with them. When you are a child, you have to get someone to do everything for you because you aren't big enough. The child is constantly pursued by the questions: Am I doing all right? Am I holding my end up? When you hold your end up as an adult, you don't question it, you know it. There's something radically wrong there. I can remember these things very clearly. The mind of a young child is a gold mine. If you want to see where the main event is, just look there.

The newborn infant only has wriggling and crying to signal that it wants something. The infant's mind frame is one in which it knows of nothing but itself. Everything is itself—the room, the world, the people—and it is the source of its own fulfillment. In the best situation, the mother figure, whoever is taking care of the child, has to be someone who doesn't have an inner revulsion to expressions of individuality. Most do and cannot tolerate individuality, because it reminds them of the fact that they were not allowed individuality.

If the mother figure has a positive attitude toward the child, and with experience is sensitive to the child's needs and wants and provides them, then the child starts off life with acquiring the attitude of achieving success in what it wants. This attitude forms the basis for the rest of life. It can form an attitude of being the one in control, of getting what it wants. That is the whole issue, and it starts at the very beginning.

This isn't spoiling the child. You cannot spoil a child. What people call spoiling a child is the parent forcing the child into the desires of the parent, and these are the ones he's allowed to have. It is forcing the child to put all his desires into a particular pattern the parent decides upon. That's why the "spoiled child" always has fits and tantrums. It is because he is forced into a false self and is not allowed to be his real self. You cannot fulfill a false self. The spoiled child occurs from coddling and creating desires that are not real in the child. They are fantasies and are only real in the parent's own mind. The child is only allowed to want what the parents want it to want. That's the whole problem in a nutshell. The kid never gets what he wants, but only what he was allowed to want. After a while he no longer knows what he wants, and only frustration remains.

It all starts in the mind-set of the person tending the child. If they can't tolerate "joie de vivre!" — let go and let go, let her rip! The rage to live... If they can't tolerate it — and almost none of them can tolerate — then they just put a pillow on the child's face, no matter what it looks like, and that's the end of that.

Parents beat their children because doing so is very well learned. They've spent their entire life beating themselves. You can't really separate between yourself and the child. There's no real guilt or pain involved in it, because in your inner mind you are chastising yourself — for things, I might add, the child may not have even done. You project some failure of your own into the pattern, you never see it objectively.

The reason we are so long in raising children is that their brain has not developed the ability to answer to themselves. You are actually an effective part of their brain. You have to do their thinking for them, because they don't have the ability to do it themselves. It is a tremendous and terrible task.

You have a child, and the child is sick and you do not recognize the sickness, as was the case with me. The child from that person cannot experience release from the sickness. The child hungers for the release from its sickness without knowing that it is the need for the other person's mind in its life, to help it do what it can't do yet. The child without exception is being denied the presence of another person in them, and they in the other. Honorably to do so is the right thing for the child. Honorably is the big word.

The child by design sees itself as others see it. If the child is seen as good and well, the child sees itself as good and well. Most of us darn near had none of being seen as good and well. The result is that most of us carry an unnamed burden throughout our lives. It generates the sense that there is something wrong here. The question of there being something wrong here is what ends up being answered to.

The work of childhood is play. The minute the play doesn't have that genuine sparkle and vivacity, they are off the track. It has to be an on-going and constant thing because the child cannot stand the frustration. Children keep dealing with something until it is over. Many traumas that occur in childhood aren't retained as psychological difficulties, but resolved right as they happen. Most serious traumas are post-pubescent.

It doesn't take much positive reinforcement in the average child for them to reach the point of feeling good about themselves. But if one runs into a negative aura in the father or mother, if the parent is the type of person who is so upset that they can't want to give the attention that is needed, they can't want to and there's nothing they can do about it. The child will spend its life

BURNS

for an acceptance that even if it finds,
l them up. I call this negative impression
hild "imprinting." Imprinting is an over-
subconscious determining factor.

e thing about people who are really divorced from themselves is that they possess an
almost psychic ability, being careful by what I
mean by psychic. They know how to hurt. They
are able through the bond that exists between
parents and children, for instance, to be sensitive to when an action on their part will hurt the
most. They will pick the moment when you are
ripe and hit you. It is uncanny.

An odd thing is that female to male imprinting is seldom accomplished, but when it is, it
is very obvious. The female needs the constant
presence and acceptance of a male figure. The
female, in my mind, is never capable of self-
determination. It is always through the male
figure. It is because of their dependent role, I
think. I think it is chemical.

When I see a woman who is headstrong, self-
determined, independent, this is all hostility in
my mind. The difference between arrogance and
humility is hostility in anybody. In women it is
hostility over the fact that they never felt wanted
securely by their male imprinters. It could be
a father, an older brother, an uncle. The odd
thing about it is that this state can transpire in
a woman for forty years, and then they find a
man, and it can completely turn around, which
is the unusual thing about it. I've seen it happen
several times. Unlike men, they can turn around.

Steve!
*
about

If men do not get a favorable imprint by the time they are two years old, there's nothing you can do about it. If a man doesn't get favorably imprinted as a child, he ends up constantly trying to control his environment. They are motivated by a desire to "engineer" in people. They want to be the pope.

If you haven't spent a minimum of fifty hours thinking about the mother-child relationship, you aren't going to have a nickel's worth of sense about what is really going on. You can't understand psychology until you understand the mother-child relationship. You see yourself as others see you, period. That is what the mother-child relationship is all about. If you don't get treated right from the start, you never get started. It doesn't matter if you live to be a hundred, or what any therapist can do. If it isn't done right in the beginning, it's never done right. It starts with the first minute of birth and probably before.

Ideally, when the infant demonstrates that it wants something to change in its environment, someone is there who understands what the child wants and sees that the child gets it. Mostly at the beginning, this is physical manipulation. Importantly the person responsible to the child should be someone who does not have a deep-seated objection to independence, their own or anybody else's. It's all there in the first six months for most people. If the string of ego reinforcement, ego encouragement, ego building, and ego support is broken at anytime between then and thirty, you are still in trouble. That's how precarious it is. Nobody will make it through if it isn't—and people talk of a "beneficent God!"

The child-like state is the state that every human alive is trying to get to. When I was about twelve, I came to the conclusion that adults were insane. They were as rammy as billy goats, and so is everyone I've ever met. Until I meet an adult with the flowering feeling and drive of a young child, I will know I've never met a sane person. There is a big difference between childish and child-like. The general state of consciousness of the child is a state that we would label euphoric. The child avoids any training that tries to burst his balloon. In our education system, all so-called learning is imposed upon the kids from without, and they hate it. If the desire to learn something comes from within, the kid will devour whatever it is.

School was totally divorced from my questions. That's why I hated it. I had so many unanswered questions that I was hanging from the ceiling by my toenails. In my last year of high school, I didn't go to five classes. I'd come to school two classes late, and then hang out in the hall and smoke a pack of cigarettes. A Catholic Brother would then come out and tell me I had another million years of detention. I could pass the tests, but couldn't stand sitting in some class with some guy telling me how important an apostrophe was in a sentence, while meanwhile I'm feeling like my insides are falling out. I had no one to talk to, so I had to get my answers from the inside. I was an excellent student until I got into this, and then I didn't care if the place burned down. To me, I had to totally understand everything I studied. I didn't memorize. I had to follow my own master. There was absolutely nothing in this world I could permit to be more important.

I escaped into my mind from a world I couldn't stand. I forced myself to think. I started out with a blank page, and everyone who comes up with something new does the same thing. I learned to notice when something important went by in my mind. I stopped everything, even if it took hours, to track it back down and follow it up. After a year or so of this, I never missed anything. I came to the conclusion that I had to find all my answers from within, that I wasn't going to get them from anyone else.

People were making me so miserable that I had to learn what made their heads tick. I had to do it with no fantasy involved and strictly and clearly see what made them operate. At the time, I had never heard the word "psychology." I had never heard of Freud. When I fully understood people to my own satisfaction—and still it brought about no relief—it caused my inner death. I went to the other side.

Sometimes analysts claim that people or children imagine that they were abused, and that this is the source of their problems. No one ever imagines they were abused. There could be a family of sixteen kids with only one who became a psychiatric patient. All the psychiatrist would say is that it was genetic. It wouldn't be genetic; he was the one who was used. He was the one who got all of the kicks. I can never be convinced that anyone can imagine that they were abused. If it is a hundred to one of people saying that he had a good home and the like, it's not possible that he wasn't abused.

# Psychology

No one virtually wants to leave home in a real sense and ever has. There's no one who reaches the point totally of saying: "All right. I'm me. I've got my capabilities and abilities, and I'm going to go out and take a crack at it alone." There is an ego conflict in this never wanting to leave home in a deeper sense. A twenty-five or thirty-year old can't face the reality that he doesn't want to leave home, but it can never be overcome until it is acknowledged. The ego conflict becomes unbearable. You don't find this mentioned by Jung, Freud, or anywhere. It is the trauma of not wanting to leave home on a subliminal level, at whatever age, and that is what it is all about. If you achieved maturity in a properly supportive environment, you'd want to leave home so badly and sow your own oats, that you couldn't wait to get out.

In puberty, the chemistry changes to the extent where you have the ongoing new ability to realize that a question exists. You had questions before puberty but did not think a thing about them. The need to know oneself is the thing that frames how success can come to a person in the different age brackets of life. When you're eighteen you are locked into one set of questions, when twenty-six it is another set, when thirty-five another, and forty, fifty, and sixty other sets. It's a matter of chemistry, and like it or not, you have to pay the fiddler.

When you're in your forties or there about, you figure you're going to change the world. Most guys get a new wife, in their mind if nothing else. They get another job, a fresh start. They tell themselves, "If they only knew then what they know now!" This is all generated by chemistry, and everybody gets into it. When fifty comes, a different stage starts. You internalize the whole thing and make apologies for every mistake you ever made, even though you may have resolved it at the time. If it wasn't for this process at fifty, we'd never have a readable book. The fifties stage is actually a review for oneself.

After forty or forty-five, if you are close enough to a person, they are able to let their hair down a bit and let you know where they are at and able to respond to personal questions. You'll find most are into improving their occupation and maintaining their place in the world. That is where their time is spent. After this age, they go through their mid-life crisis and it is a different story.

When a person goes mad, in one way, he loses his imaging process. He no longer has his mind's eye. You don't know what this is until you lose it. A good psychiatrist would say that you burned out and went on automatic. When a normal person gets excessively tired, the imaging ability disappears. This will happen to anybody. You go on automatic. You no longer participate in your own thoughts. Your thoughts are going on but you don't experience them mentally. It is a type of split in consciousness and hell on earth.

Some wives and mothers develop a split that manifests in every word coming out of their mouth breaking down to "Look what you've done to me!" They are usually hypochondriacs. They will never admit it, but think just the opposite of what they say, which is true schizophrenia. They have two mind-sets going simultaneously, one conscious, the other unconscious. True schizophrenia has nothing to do with duality in personality. This split in people's consciousness is the commonest reality and is really what schizophrenia is. Psychiatrists and psychologists act like it isn't there and give another, different, definition to schizophrenia.

The problem of current psychology you meet in institutions, is that they only deal with certain areas of dysfunction such as memory and recall. That's all they are interested in. They aren't interested in describing the underlying process. They have abandoned it. They don't describe general mind-sets behind problems. They just say, "This is a dysfunction." Today's definition of insanity is "Do you pay the bills?" Period.

Every time an analyst can't get anywhere with someone, he does the same thing most people do—he decides it's all your fault. Whenever an analyst labels someone a goldbrick, it just means they don't want to or can't get to the root of the problem and don't want to put up with the person. No matter how they describe it, what in essence they say is that a person is not getting better because he is some sort of goldbricker or malingerer. I think what the case really is, is that they just couldn't cope with them. The analyst doesn't know what to do. What it comes down to is: we can't account for why this guy got this attitude; we don't know what to do with this attitude; and we have beaten our heads against this attitude and gotten nowhere. Where every psychiatrist shuts a person off is that he wants to be important to them, yet he won't allow the person to be important to him. It's one-sided, unnatural, and won't work.

A psychiatrist's sanity is threatened every day, but they still keep at it. You cannot imagine what it is like to be in a sea of despair like a mental hospital. You never see a smile. You never hear a laugh. You never hear two intelligible, sensible words. A psychiatrist is a person with enough intelligence to get through medical school, yet without exception they have no friends. They have no contacts. The only people they see are people who can't find their way to the bathroom. You can't constantly take that type of environment. People live by having peer groups, by being understood and valued. Each person that comes to see him basically wants to destroy everything in sight.

Because of all the inner frustration in mental hospitals, the psychiatrists are so overloaded with all the projections of the patients on them that they live in fear. If I were to frame it in Freudian terms, it would be the Oedipal Complex. They do everything in their power to form a chemical lobotomy on the patients, which prevents the patients from a genuine experience of themselves, in the hope that some dissolution of this frustrated energy will occur to allow them to walk safely on the grounds. So long as a person is on drugs, he cannot do introspection at all. Psychotherapy with a person on drugs does absolutely no good, absolutely none. Drugs separate the inner and outer selves. The only drug that doesn't have this effect is lithium.

Psychiatrists have no idea how drugs work. When they say they have some idea of how it works on the brain, they're only talking about the output from the patient who is taking the drug. They're not talking about the actual chemistry and mechanics of the brain. If you have a chemical that is able to affect the brain, you are getting close to something the brain is able to do by itself by design. If it was not, you wouldn't be able to have the effect. This dimension is truly being run, in my view, from a stable position of superior knowledge that we can't generally have insight into. We are generally and mostly not here in this dimension, but we are familiar with it and we accept it as being here. My honest thought is that the real programmer is on the other side. The DNA is left here only as a vehicle. I have to think that actually we never get here fully. If you are to consider that our body may have descended from an ape, to be here in perfect spirit you would have to have a perfected form to contain it. I honestly feel we don't completely get here. Some of us get here, more or less at various times, but we truly don't reside here because the job isn't done.

Before psychiatrists came along, people went to ministers. Ministers probably had the same success rate as psychiatrists but for much less money. I have minister friends who endlessly bemoan this fact. Something that really throws a wrench into it all for me is that every psychiatrist I've known and gotten to the point of talking about it, has said that they wouldn't have become a psychiatrist if they knew what they were getting into. When I ask them why, they say, "I can't do anything else!" Several have said this to me.

In my twenties, I began questioning what was worth doing if I could do it. I learned that certain things drew me out. I was drawn to mechanical things. I was drawn to music. I was drawn to a few pieces of poetry. After awhile I began to understand the movements in others, where I could see similar movements. Then I burned out and moved into the dark world. It was an entirely different world, and I've lived in it, more or less ever since. In the past few years things have changed somewhat and I've had an opportunity to compare the two.

Most people in mental hospitals are not burned out as I was. Their conscious mind still functions. Some are in an endless conversation with what I don't know. They are always talking to themselves. Occasionally, the scan of their comprehension will include you when you're there, but only peripherally, and only to a minimum. Their delusion is totally irrational and usually relates to nothing that has any sense to it at all. There's about ten percent of the population in mental hospitals I've seen that are roughly in that state. It takes great knowledge, wide reading, and practical experience to get any response out of them about anything. They don't want to relate to people at all. You have to be able to second guess at what is going on in their mind. You have to be an authority figure to them to be able to get any response at all. If you seem an ordinary person like themselves, they won't pay any attention to you. The ordinary inmate of a mental institution has complete disdain for everybody on earth with good reason.

When a person gets mentally sick, it has nothing to do with anything that would commonly come to the mind of a healthy person who is trying to understand. A "heal thyself" person trying to understand doesn't have a chance because the sick mind generates a reality that the healthy mind has no access to, has no experience of, has no notion of. It's a filthy state.

When you are mentally healthy, your mind is on what you are doing and what is in front of you. When you are sick, no matter what you are doing, you aren't thinking about it. You are not conscious of the state you are in. You're in a state and can't get out of it. Usually you don't know you are getting sick. Your inner mind knows but you don't. After years of sickness, you realize that the world is hostile to you, but you don't care. You realize you don't have any interest in anything, but you don't care.

Until recently I was pistol whipped. What I mean by this is that there was nothing left in me with which to complain about what had happened to me. I used to scream and rave about what my situation was, but it was all hollow. It was like screaming about being in chains, with no capacity to get rid of the chains. I don't know how to describe it except I used to call it "screaming against the restraint." I was broken, there wasn't a whimper left in me, and all the hooting was an empty barrel rolling down the hill. It was just noise—there wasn't anything in it for me. I could not stop doing it, but I didn't get anything out of it. Because of something that happened, this all changed in an instant. It didn't take five seconds.

There is a great diversity in mind experience in people, and you cannot walk two roads at once. Everybody comes to their state of knowing by the experiences that they have had. While they are largely similar, there are also vast differences. So you have to know someone for a long time in order to explain their behavior in terms that are meaningful to you, if only to yourself and not to them. When he does such and such, I perceive it as such and such. On this side, you'll never have the opportunity to take it any further. You can't get inside the other person and know whether it is a decent match. The odds are that it might not be, because you did not grow up in the same moment-to-moment experience that they did.

A particular reaction to our present society is cults. In my view cultists are a type of person who have become utterly disgusted with the ordinary of life. They give up entirely on the ordinary mainstream of life and find someone who can produce serenity in their mind. They've suffered so much upset that they throw over the ordinary ways of everything they've known in life.

What they are seeking is an auto-hypnotic state. They don't know a thing about seeking, but they have seen the people in cults in what I'd call a "stuperous" state. They sense and intuit what that state is and they want it. It is a weird thing. The cause of it is in someone's previous home life. Pain made them go into a cult. Boredom doesn't have anything to do with it. It's pain to the point of panic from disillusionment. They never had a happy experience and it is better to leave them alone than to put them back in that same situation.

The cultist has to be impressionable. A street-smart person doesn't end up in a cult. They still have to be looking for "big daddy" without thinking of it as big daddy. They have a knot in their stomach and can't stand the view of life their family has generated and fostered on them. That view makes life look like hell-fire and brimstone, which it is when they are in that state. Somebody comes along then and says, "All you have to do is shave your head, wear a robe, stand on the corner, and say Um-a-Um-a-Um-a-Um-abba and I'll take care of you forever." The thing that amazes me is that there are any kids that *aren't* in a cult.

You wouldn't believe what conversation with a cultist is like—circles of logic every ten seconds. That's the only way that state can be maintained. They have to keep repeating the "mantra," and the mantra is one day long. They've got enough gibberish stuffed into themselves to keep themselves away from their selves for one twenty-four hour period, and they go at it one day at a time. Repetition is the root of the capability to be able to maintain the state. A fanatic cannot hear you and what you have to say if they tried. The circle of logic they've worked out and dwell in keeps them from the pain in their consciousness. It is auto-hypnotic, and they are programmed to think certain thoughts that evade all emotion. They are very carefully worked out programs of thought. There's still a fire underneath, so they have to keep at it.

Hubbard and Scientology are dangerous. Hubbard discovered it is possible to, what I call "get on a plateau." It's a method of getting away from the problem and escaping into something else. Scientology is about nothing but controlling the electrical potential reaction from your hands on the "E-meter." When there is no reaction to things, you are supposed to be "clear." What you are is completely disconnected from things, hypnotized. It's dangerous. If you want to see a zombie, see a "clear" Scientologist. They've completely separated their comprehension from their driving process. Intellect has to be connected with feeling through comprehension or you create a monster.

Two thousand years ago, people did not understand hypnotism, but they used it. They did not have sharp, clear concepts about hardly anything. They were just beginning to learn tools, crafts, trades. The only people with sharp, clear minds about anything were the carpenters, the potters, the stone masons, the builders. They're the only people who had to be able to reproduce things exactly. The common horde was doing nothing but following sheep around and tilling the earth and didn't have to have sharp concepts. You bring into this someone who has a native capacity for thinking—which I consider to be genetic, like Christ, who in my view was basically a hypnotist—and they could produce a big effect.

Somebody in those times could be taken and put into a trance and they'd never know there was a trance. I put people into a trance by talking, but I tell them about it. I put them into a trance in the area of reality where resolution takes place. There are a million frames of mind available. I'm referring to the one in which resolution takes place. It is hypnotic, but it works.

Anybody at that time could come into a mob of people and start talking "reality," and the reaction would be like the first time someone heard a symphony. They either hated it or loved it. Generally, they hated it because it was so new and foreign. I'm referring to someone who comes along with a particular brand of mumbo jumbo.

What happens, I claim, is that all human beings from birth have a definite need of a spiritual experience, but a spiritual experience is relative. Anyone who can come in front of them and say, "I am a messiah," turns them on and gives them a feeding in a part of their psyche that they have been languishing with since they were born. They come away illuminated and they don't even know what happened. They could never repeat the experience themselves. That's how I see the type of thing that went on. It was feeding a hunger.

If you've had time to analyze communication, you notice that you may hear one thing but came away with a different impression. Communication is a total thing. The least dependable and accurate part of it is the spoken word. You have to be there and accept how little you really know about the person before you. It takes time. In total communication, you are very slow on words and very long on the feelings people generate in you. If you can develop the ability to be aware of what is in someone else's mind, it will enhance the ability to be aware of what is in your own mind.

After the bridge between the inner and outer self has been destroyed, so that consciously you do not experience the inner being much if at all, then the experience of love must go through the back door. Most of the love in the world today that we experience is indirect. It is mostly because that love is so strong that it'll burn the inner circuits if the bridge between the inner and outer you is not strong enough. If the bridge is absent, washed out, you cannot experience the thing from below into the consciousness.

The result is that most return of the expression of love comes to the surface after a long period of time. I have friends whom I've known all my life who have a great deal of feeling for me. I say feeling and not love because it cannot generate into the remembered feeling of the teenage years when love was a very real and tangible thing and most often unanswered to. The result is that most love is now simply the ability to accept someone's need to be as nutty as you are.

People want to love more than they want to be loved. The more you pay attention to a person, the more you are siphoning off love. The worse frustration on this earth is not not being loved, but not being allowed to love. People won't let you near them. Everyone is trying so desperately to keep their own boat afloat, that when someone else injects their presence, they reject it because they need the time and presence of themselves so badly. You have to be sneaky. Considering the spans of time that we know of — if you can imagine someone living a thousand years ago, which is no time at all — there wasn't time for someone to even begin to consider inner and outer selves because of the difficulty of just surviving. We've definitely come a long way when you think in terms of thousands of years. If you have a belly-ache now, and have to get up and go to work anyway, and can't answer to the inner pain, the result is that the mind shuts off.

Then you get into what I call "automatic" with a vague sense of the inner self that is the most common condition of the vast number of people today.

For various reasons we have built cities, but we do not have the vaguest sense of the psychological problems that are involved in them. We build our houses so closely together that we cannot escape the expressive envelope of every house on the street. You become accustomed to it.

If you walk by a house, a person, or a bus goes by, no matter how internally involved you are in your own thoughts, you are constantly presented with the question "Why is that not right?" When you walk by a house and the porch is in disarray, the grass isn't cut and the like, your innate sensitivity for beauty and order is violated. Consider the state of the cities and consider that every aspect of turmoil, of frustration, is expressed nonverbally in the state of consciousness of the mass of the people. They do not know what they are doing or why, yet your sensitivity is constantly there and you are constantly required to answer to it.

You may start a day feeling pretty well and things are going good, but in the course of the day you run into a few people who subtly upset you, and wish you hadn't had the experience you had with them. It might have been mild negative experiences, strong ones, or anything in between. Our goal here is to be at a state of familiarity with self so consistently, that the instant you meet someone and something doesn't go right—or something does go right—that you know why that response is there, what it's all about, and what it means to you. You can run into a bus driver who will upset the heck out of you. What do you do when this happens all the time? There are a lot of such people in the world. What do you do when you've had so much bad experience with people that you no longer ever want to see what is out there? You are so sick of looking at these people that you could just go to some fantasy land and live there forever. Basically, that's all that mental illness is—bad experience. All graduations of it come from having to deal with people who just didn't have what you needed. There are things you have to have from others, and if you can't get them you are in trouble. You end up being rejected, negative, abandoned, and any one of the series of descriptions used.

We desire to be free of hatred. One of the most energy consuming and damning things on earth is hatred. But if you don't answer to it face to face, you'll never escape it. If we ever get to the point where we have mastered living well enough to do it with internal harmony, then we will have the time in every day, with the company of one another, to come to the release of the tensions in one another. It is our deepest drive. We not only desire to release our own tensions, *we are all one*, and are of necessity required to release the tension in those around us. I was out looking for someone to pay attention to me, and

I found the way to do it was to pay attention to them. That's where the relief is.

The false self is the difference between what you want to do and what you are allowed to do. I remember when all I had to do to get rid of my friends was to let my real feelings show on my face, and they were like the cockroaches going for the corners. That was the first real relief I ever had after three or four years of struggle. It then dawned on me that every son of a gun who had ever gone down the road, who ever saw this thing for what it was, went straight through where I just went through.

The point people fail to realize is that if you are true to yourself, you're alone, and you will do anything to avoid the experience of being abandoned. That's the whole circle of life. Whole societies demonstrate one side of the issue. The Japanese have no tolerance of independence. They stultify all of the things that go together to make up self-determination, strength of character, strength of will, strength of energy and force, locus of self in the propulsion forward to find answers to your wants. They stultify all of them. Their society is still feudally oriented. They are successful at what they do because they operate as one mind. They have a national consciousness. They do not have private consciousnesses. It is like a beehive with all the prices of the beehive.

Every person who ever accomplished anything—and it is always one individual who accomplishes anything because masses of people don't make breakthroughs—would have far rather been dead if he could have gotten away with it. It isn't worth it in any respect. It takes a crucifixion to generate an inner experience. How does this reflect on the notion that God is a loving being and all that clap-trap? I can only conclude that some people think that way because for them life must be a pleasant experience. But what about the people for whom it isn't? People get to the point where they're so separated from themselves that they want to destroy the whole darn world, which is the thrust of everything that leads to warfare. The whole direction of the nuclear problem is the desire for self-destruction. If you can step away from it all and see it for what it is, why would anyone play with something like nuclear bombs, knowing that most people are crazy? If some son of a gun gets a bad fried egg in the morning, the whole thing might go up. You wouldn't do this in a rational state, but this is the state we are in. We have a world full of people wandering around in a fog.

I wouldn't try to convince anyone, but it is my opinion that we have many lives. Something came up in my mind the other day, and I said to myself, "Well, maybe she was right." I was remembering a woman at an A.R.E. meeting a long time ago who had looked at me with eyes like saucers and said, "You devil. You devil!" She claimed she saw that I had been a slave trader in a previous existence, and that's why I'm having such a hard time of it this time around. If you start believing such stuff, though, you're so far in trouble you'll never get out. Mostly it is believed by people with no practical ego.

When you start looking at yourself, you are looking at blind feelings. You have been dealing with blind feelings for years because they weren't allowed in the environment you are in, and this is the problem. The point is not to go with your feelings, but to understand what is behind them. The last guy that "went with his feelings" is doing life for murder. People are like boiling kettles all the time, but become so accustomed to it that they regard it as normal. This is the "shadow side" of a person in Jungian terminology. It is what is trying to get these feelings to the surface.

I don't see Jung's "shadow side" as being something normal. I don't think there is anything intrinsically negative in the human psyche, but because we don't know how to answer to it, it gets frustrated. Only in the presence of it becoming bottled up does it become negative. I might add that that is after years of it.

The first thing that comes up upon a negative reaction of the psyche is that the person says, "That can't be me!" I always knew it was me. Some days, a friend I would meet in the morning would ask, "How's it going?" I'd tell him, "I just came from the house and shaved the devil!" I would have just finished looking at a guy in the mirror, red-faced and with eyes bulging from being in a rage, and I knew it was me.

If there is one single, starting, repeating, endlessly-to-be-learned-about function in my description of the reality of the mind, it is that everything you do circles around your chief hang-up. You are always talking about it in interrelationships with other people. One of the first things you have to learn to study is how your body responds when you meet somebody. Your body is never wrong. You might want to run away. If you do like them, you want to stay. That is the key. If you meet someone and get a stomach ache, that's the bodily response to get to the root of. Sometimes you repress it and get the reaction the next day.

When you have someone who has been affected by something all their life, but has never been able to get enough distance between themselves and the negative experience to identify what it did to their mind-set and outlook, then the whole situation manifests in a bodily response. Also, everything you don't come to terms with, is still there, and occupying a portion of your conscious energy in circles. In the bodily response, our technique here is to meet the bodily response to a thought, feeling, situation, or trauma. Bring it to the surface as clearly as possible. Hold it in consciousness as long as possible and you can stand it. Permit it to generate a new view of what's causing the problem. That's the root of the whole technique. The more effective you are in dealing with feelings, the sharper your comprehension becomes. The better you are in dealing with your inner homework, the better you are at everything.

The key to success in this whole process is that you never have the same emotion twice.

What you're trying to do in this process is to get the patterns that you've identified as being repetitive and a blind end, to go further, to move on, to change, and to blossom into a new insight.

Every habit pattern that you've identified as being repetitive and static is a hammer beating at your consciousness, trying to get you to move forward. The more common the habit is, the more easily it can be opened up, as contradictory as that may seem. If you want to decide where to start your effort, pick the most repetitive habit you have, that you know is off key. That's where the most energy is. And where the energy is at is the key to where the problem is.

When you open it up, you won't believe the flood of insight that it will bring. Your other brain channels and synapses have all been worked way forward in consciousness, but held back at that point. If it's not something that is deep, anything that is deep that is related to it is immediately accessible. The minute you knock that wall down and move one inch forward, you're in a new universe. You have all the energies and drives immediately at hand to open and expand the world that you brought yourself into.

You can't start anywhere else other than where your real problem is. What happens is that you can't deal with anything else regardless. Every emphasis that is going on in your mind on the subliminal and subconscious level is related to it. You think you're doing something else, but you're not. If you're not on the right track, you can't get the right answer.

The unconscious is suppressed conscious capability. The ability was there if it had been answered to, to have been aware of it in the conscious mind. The unconscious is the large body of unanswered opportunities to answer questions. The need was there. The question was generated, but it wasn't answered to. I separate between that dimension and the true subconscious, which can only generally be reached through the meditative process. The subconscious is the generator, in my experience. I had to answer to the unconscious to the point where it would give me five minutes off, and then get into the subconscious to determine what direction it wanted to go in. I would answer to that, and when that was done, I would automatically find myself in the super conscious, which was the point of my thrust in the first place.

I've been on the super conscious side of things many times in this life, and if it wasn't for that fact—if I hadn't had the perspective of timeless things—I simply couldn't have done it and maintained the ability to stay on the street. It's as simple as that. The habit pattern in my life has been to answer first to the sore stomach. If I try not to, and go to work, I become completely incapacitated. I can't even think. It's simply because of sane circumstances, I had the opportunity to go within earlier on. When your system develops the ability to get some satisfaction in the inner arena, it becomes master. You can't control it. It won't listen to the street necessities. It won't pay attention to them.

I don't wait ten seconds before I let everyone I meet know that I've been in a mental institution. I don't waste ten seconds before I clear the air, and then it is gone. The reason is because of something that has happened several times. People have said to me, "I thought you were the most insightful person I ever met, until I heard you were in a mental institution." To heck with that.

Practice at free association is the only practice I know of, if you are lucky enough to be able to submit to the pressure of it, to be prepared for what comes when something forces the valve open of a kundalini experience. In my experience, the kundalini starts in the chest, although at the time I didn't know the word "kundalini." It has nothing to do with sex. Your conscious mind is incapable of letting anything unknown into it. By allowing free association, you get accustomed to shock.

Fantasizing is caused by the inner urge to go beyond what your conscious mind is accustomed to or allowed. Your fantasies are constantly trying to awaken you to the feeling of being motivated, if it is about being a concert pianist or whatever. Most people reach a point where they say, "This is all B.S." and shut it down and destroy what good it does them.

The ultimate basis for sexuality, and even sexual fantasy if it were possible to get behind it—which it isn't for virtually anyone—is the drive for all comprehension. My view of sex is that a bed is for sleeping. In the mental realm, sexuality does not exist. It ceases to exist. People have been looking for an answer in sex for the last million years and no one has found one yet. On the other hand, to me celibacy means staying away from women, which seems about as wrong as you can get. Nearly all the sex urge is not genital at all if you experience the depth beyond the superficial. Real libido is beyond the false libido of sex.

When you get into the area of sex, you should have real feeling for the person, an accurate identification of their good points and their bad points, and a genuine desire to be with them that is separate from the specific area of lust. In normal sex, a similar phenomenon is going on as in anger. Real sex is quite a different thing. If you can come to the point of realizing that the only freedom comes from mutual need, if that becomes the basis of all your sexual experience, you reach the point of having sex darn near never. This is because you'll only do it when it is good, when you learn what good is, and when the time is right. I have fought with the concept of sublimation of energy since the first day I heard of it. I do not think it is possible. You advance the whole front. You don't take something out of here and put it over there.

It is good to learn to clarify your appetites. Don't eat until you know exactly what you want to eat. Don't eat fast. Don't eat in noisy environments. Get as much bodily participation or response out of everything you do as you can possibly get, starting with food, because it is the most common. You will begin to realize the difference of habit with real appetite. Almost nobody eats when they are hungry. They eat because it is there, or it's time. People eat to numb themselves out, to prevent consciousness. In blunting the basic experience of real appetite, you destroy the capacity to be razor sharp in identifying any of the urges that arise from your blind or shadow side. If you follow this simple practice, you'll see what value is in it.

People talk of being physically drained, but there is no such thing as being physically drained. To feel drained is something different than feeling physically tired. You have to take a very close look at the distinction. If you feel drained, it's because you are not doing what your soul wants. If you're not doing what your soul wants, you're going to feel drained from doing nothing to everything. Until you know exactly what turns your spark of interest on, until you know exactly what it is and are engaged in it, you are going to be drained at the end of every day. It doesn't matter how many authorities disagree with this, it is still a fact. If you find something that is fulfilling, don't wander away from it.

When you are doing what your soul wants to do, you'll have so much energy you won't know what to do with it. If it is in the mental realm, you have to balance it by doing something physical to bring the body chemistry back into equilibrium. You will start head tripping if you don't. You have to do something physical to bring yourself back down. Locations have something to do with this also. There's such a thing as not being able to be your true self in certain locations or places associated with negative experiences. In dreams, you go to the locations or settings where you can be your true self.

Your inner side is always trying to bring these things to your attention. Paranoia is another method, and is not delusion but your inner mind trying to get you to pay attention to something, and it won't stop until you bite the bullet. Hearing voices is another example. Voices are a person's own self, and if you could demonstrate that, it would be the end of voices. I know. I've been down that road. The belief in entities comes from the same source as the desire for the perfectly fulfilled person to come and guide you.

I'm a mechanic, and for two and a half years haven't been able to tell what is wrong with my car. For two and a half years, I spent every dime out of pocket, every dime of psychic energy, and I'm sick. I'm trying to demonstrate something here about when something keeps hankering at a person. Someone said to me about it, "You know better. It's not the car that's got you upset, it's the symbol."

The minute I realized that, my inner side saw an opportunity to have a field day with me, and make me feel like an idiot because I couldn't solve the problem. My inner side is always looking for an opportunity to make me feel like an idiot. Why? I have never had a job. I have never had a family. I don't have a house. I don't have any ego. I constantly have to live with this side that can't stop railing at me. The reason this is important is that everyone has three, at least, people to live with. You, a child, and the less-than-ego.

Comprehension is a compulsion, and the mind needs to know just as the body needs to have certain things. The only thing that releases you from inner stress are explanations that hold water. Comprehension is a functional thing that is affected by all the things around it. You're under barrage from countless inputs, and you're continually filtering them to determine the best and simplest route to your own satisfactions, including mental satisfactions. You *need* to see pretty flowers. You need to see the country. You need to see the city, which amazes me.

The average person learns constantly, but they only learn successfully if they don't notice it. If you notice it consciously, you have to go through ego death. The ego doesn't have one bit of sense it can't give up. You can't check out no matter what the problems. Whenever you come upon something you need to know, you go through an ego death, because the ego can never admit it needs to know anything. If you learn to become clever and effective at ego death, you can really streamline the process. You still have to go through it every time, you cannot circumvent it.

Consciousness is at the crossroads of desire and fulfillment, and is allowed to work as long as it gets the job done. If it doesn't, the whole house of cards comes down. When your consciousness doesn't get what it needs, it disintegrates. Ego is intrinsically involved in this, so the ego dies also. If you can't get what you need out of your environment, you're done, consciousness quits.

Ego is a very phony, slippery, and difficult thing to get hold of. Everything is "I did," and the truth is that you don't do anything. You are a victim of your circumstances, but at a certain point your need for identity takes over and you say, "I did, I thought. I this and I that." In my opinion we are at the crossroads of being. We have nothing to do with how things got here or where they are going. If you really examine the thing, you are just sitting in a theatre while this is taking place. You are where it happened, and that's about all you have to do with it. The truth is that in the larger sense there is no choice. We are continually making choices based on determining all the chances in different areas. But if you had the ability to be conscious of all the factors, there wouldn't be any choice. Choice in the small sense and choice in the large sense are very tricky areas.

# Philosophy, Mysticism, and The Other Side

I used to spend most of my thinking time on cosmology. The whole effort is an attempt to escape the truth that life is a madhouse from beginning to end. To be clearly conscious of what the world is like is agony. I've never seen anyone who got to the point of having disdain for life ever reverse their attitude. A process goes on progressively from birth to death. Some call it "wising up," but another thing to call it is "accepting defeat." It is defeat. Your fantasies die one at a time. Most people die physically before they get to the point of total rejection. Nobody goes the other way. Nobody gets happier and happier.

Real philosophy is different from scholastic philosophy, which—after Plato—is ninety-eight percent horse manure. It is a particular form of insanity, delusions of grandeur gone wild on a paying basis. Scholastic philosophers make psychologists look like healthy men. They put out pure garbage devoid of any capacity to experience meaning. You wind up feeling like you are chewing cotton.

I started in pre-Law in college. Law has absolutely nothing to do with anything. All these cases are decided by manic lawyers who are having a good day and sway the judges. It is all theatre. When I eventually saw through it, I had to get out. In my first five minutes of a philosophy class, I knew I had discovered where I belonged. I later learned that scholastic philosophers were nuttier than psychologists. Everything but philosophy is child's play. No one would settle for dandelions when they know what roses are.

We have the essential assumption that we are on a trip from unknowing to all-knowing. All religions and cosmologies are different versions of this same theme. It's the underlying implication in all conscious effort. But how can any being be the absolute master of his own destiny, which is what it boils down to? Our type of comprehension is entirely limited. If it weren't for habit patterns, nothing would get done. But habit is the antithesis of insight. Habits block insight at every turn because it takes time to sift this idea and see what it does to that idea. By saying that our comprehension is limited, consider what would happen if we had to be attentive to the basic operation of Nature, if we had to consciously digest our food. Image if we had to be conscious of and control all this. Our comprehension is designed in limitation.

You've gone as far as comprehension can go when you get to paradox. You come to two equally opposed expressions of the situation. Most any explanation will only suffer so much examination. If you look at any explanation too closely, the whole thing will fall apart. We can use the word "infinite," for instance, and it can have sane meaning to us, but only by comparison to the fact that we presently aren't infinite. The main reason for the concept's existence is to give dimension. You cannot know black without white. It is impossible. Our structure is such that we cannot make a perception in the absence of dimension. We see all reality as patterned after our own reality, which is probably another tragic mistake in the way our minds work. You can get in trouble going too far, because our comprehension is only designed to operate in a limited range. It has to be that way or we simply couldn't survive.

Everything is an extension of the questioning process. This is the point most scientists lose track of. Why are they asking questions in the first place? Why are the questions so insufferably unanswerable no matter what they find? The reason is that they are answering the wrong questions. They are in the laboratory looking for the reason why they can't sleep, and they're never going to find the answer in the laboratory. Intellect is a monster when it is not connected in comprehension with feeling.

You may start on the trip that brings you to referring only to yourself as the source of your answers. Unknowingly accepting other people's answers through books and the like, is the trap which we are all born into our system, but there's no alternative. When growing up we have to be taught to tie our shoes. If we had to figure it out ourselves, we'd be fourteen before we figured out the bowknot.

The great danger of the written and spoken word is that you will ingest conclusions without the pain of the growth. You can't do it. It won't work. You start to read in order to learn, but the problem is that we all use the written word as an opiate, as an escape from thinking, as an escape from the pain. It is a dangerous trap because in time you are forced to resolve every issue you ever came to in the mental realm. You create a need to answer every question that is generated through the interface and interrelatedness of all these concepts.

We get into the trap of thinking that the written and spoken word have answers. They are only answers of the written and spoken word, not the questions of the body, which are injected with every word we read. When someone writes a book, you have to question what his purpose was in writing it. No one can do anything but describe themselves. It doesn't do any good to learn from a book because it's not your story. This is an entirely individualistic thing. You may listen to someone for hours and only one sentence will have a pressing meaning for you, one thing you were looking for. It has to have reference to what you are trying to do inside, whether you are conscious of it or not. You have to find concepts that release your gut tensions. Most of us go through the time of being so isolated from our gut experiences that we literally don't know that they're there. If that were not true, there would never be a day's work done.

You have an accumulated world of experience, and in being a man there is a part of you that is always trying to see how this affects that, and what does this over here mean, and how did this get to be like that. You can't stop this process and are stuck with it. Women, I think, generally don't have the ability to raise mind before the age of thirty-five because of the simple chemistry involved.

Every time you break through into a sharp, clear realization or imagery in any area, all of a sudden you set up a whole new standard, and everything you've ever thought up has to be brought up and compared with it. It's a standard process, and you have to start all over again. This occurs until you break through and achieve the awareness of *this I know is me*. When you achieve that realization, you break into the final frontier. From then on, after you've done the massive review and re-evaluation from breaking into that final frontier, everything thereafter is done for the rest of time. You don't have to do the massive revision any longer, or go over everything every time you achieve insight. I spent thirty years doing it.

I've spent a lot of my life driving. My doctor is the automobile. I'm talking about hundreds of thousands of miles. That is where I bought my silence. I've driven because it gives the outer mind just enough to do to keep it from attacking, so that the inner mind has the opportunity to come up and smell fresh air. The best thing you can do with inner problems is to get them on the surface. It might be temporary agony, but it's endless relief. It's like the sign by the side of the road, "Dig We Must For A Better Future." To be genuinely "clear" is to have answered to every question you have had to date, and I've been there on a regular basis. If that isn't paradise, I don't know what is. It is to have taken every feeling that ever entered into your comprehension and have traced it all the way back to its roots.

We are accustomed to think in the limited bag of concepts that we already have, and there is a fear to try and reach out beyond that. You will try to get something out of the bag you already have. For awhile it will fit, and then it won't fit. It will wind up making you more uneasy than you were before. You wind up getting answers that don't fit the questions.

A great problem is the fear involved in realizing that you know nothing. When I first came to the place of being able to face the unknown, I split the most difficult rock for me in my entire life. Facing the unknown takes a lot of personal quiet and divorcement from the world around you. I studied this very carefully. It is the bridge between the inner and outer man.

It takes hundreds of hours of facing the unknown to get the unknown to yield one little insight, one little piece at a time. If you are going to be any good at it, you have to be lucky enough to escape the trap of thinking that you can learn anything from books. You can learn anything at all about outside reality from a book, but when it comes to describing your inner reality, it cannot by definition ever be described by anyone else. It can only be described by you. No one else has access to it. It is a totally solo and an into-the-unknown trip.

I learned to take things to their logical extremes and see what is going on behind them. You have to deal with the problem at hand and not get a point in thought ahead of yourself. There is a perfected image behind every thought, and until you have every one of them honed to a razor edge, you can't achieve the comprehension that your soul so desperately needs. You have to get the time to develop the frontal mind to keep track of the rest of you. You have to constantly answer to questions presented to you from the environment. Everyone has questions longing to be answered inside of them, but for some reason in most people the pressure of the question isn't that great.

If you learn to go to sleep slowly, you can pick up information from the crossover state of images between waking and sleeping. I think numerology first originated from information gotten in the crossover state. Numerology doesn't have anything to do with mathematics. "0" is the state of unknowing. "1" is the state of knowledge. "2" is the state of bringing the knowledge into the practical. "3" is the state of completion—spiritual, mental, practical. "4" is dealing with the practical. "5" is the number of change. "6" is the number of the Overself or the Christ in you. "7" is the psychic number. "8" is completion as opposed to involvement in the earth. "9" is the last phase of integration of new information and completion of a cycle, and on and on. These ideas have been generating in men's minds since the beginning of time. It says more about the nature of thinking itself than anything else.

Mysticism is a continuing trend of thought and experience brought about by contemplating the nature of the organization of matter in the universe. It brings a high and sense of fulfillment that no other thinking will bring. The first philosopher I ever identified with was Plato, because I felt he had had the same experience. The source of all this world to me—and to the extent which our structures allow us to understand it—is that there is an energy, of which the most physically understandable aspect is light. This energy is slowed down. When it is slowed down to an extent, there is time and space. In the condition beyond time and space, there is only a condition in, and not a condition to question in. Our problem is our lack of ability to accelerate our being to the absence of time, the absence of motion.

People who desire a mystical experience may actually be preventing it by thinking that the urgency they feel may be for that experience, when at that point in time it may be for something completely different. You have to find a way of knowing the hunger inside of you. If you don't find a way of satisfying the hunger, you will be hard pressed to pursue anything. You have to see where accidentally you have been making efforts against your own best interests.

In an extreme form of concentration, like in motorcycle racing, a person develops attention able to be focused on about fifteen different factors at once. All the while the person is also maintaining a single overriding frame of mind. If something breaks the concentration, he better get out in a hurry. Musicians in a band also achieve this state of concentration and hear every note that is being played. They may even be aware of the state of mind of each person they are playing with. No one can stay in this state for very long. Drugs make it impossible.

When I finally became successful at deep meditation, I came to a frame of mind that was identical to this type of stream consciousness. I had the ability to be on stream totally in all levels of capacity to perceive in any sense, from physical things right down to the most abstract level of comprehension. I don't know if this would be called Cosmic Consciousness because I don't know for certain what is meant by the term. I've only had this experience once. When I try to talk to someone about the thing, I'm strapped for a description. The only way I know how to describe it is that, if you imagine your comprehension as a pinpoint in space, and from all directions around that point you are perceiving totally. It is the same function as the increased concentration in the motorcycle racer example, but about a thousand times more intense. It is being at the peak of the universe and surveying it all in comprehension.

Illumination is the opposite of the feeling of complete worthlessness. Everybody has known a time when they felt completely outcast, downtrodden, completely worthless and useless. The other extreme on that same line of experience is the feeling of being completely at one with yourself, being completely informed and capable of handling anything that you have to face, of being completely serene and beyond the capability of doubting your own capabilities and capacities. To understand this phenomenon, you can see that the concept of focus in calm consciousness is merely the focal point between internal drives and external fulfillments. In the one case where you are feeling utterly worthless, the lens of focus has fallen slack, is nothing but a pane of glass and cannot focus on anything of value either on the inside or the outside. At the other extreme, the lens is sharply focused and very clear, and able to pick up desires without any effort, and with no effort be able to find in the world the sources of fulfillment.

The most overwhelming experience I've had was the knowing of my Overself that occurred to me in my middle teens. It answered to a whole realm of my being that I had no suspicion even existed before the experience. Nothing in my Catholic education suggests that such a thing could happen to a person. I had to totally give up the sense of any personal being and take a chance that there was nothing there that would be destructive to me. Which I was able to do and did. It was a death from remorse, from failure. I literally died from it—the pressure was so great. It got me to the other side, and the minute I got there, my first question was "Did I fail?" My answer was, "You couldn't have failed if you tried to. You did a brilliant job. You went down like a valiant sailor." I haven't been bothered by failure again. I know it is a false concept. No one can fail. I feel this experience is what has carried me through the rest of my life. I know that this body will pass and I will return to that place.

The sense that first came to me was that of being free of the trap. It was a relief beyond expression here. There were different experiences in the same realm. To describe it, I can only point to the wonder of a child the night before Christmas, the inability to contain your desire to be there before you're there. Strangely, it is the simple experience of being there in the full realm of the things you experience there.

The question of returning came up and it was similar to that of my other experiences. The capacity to do generates the necessity to do. As soon as you have on the other side committed yourself, even by a slight suggestion to return, then the hunger to return is generated. In my experience, to be honest, this world is quite miserable. We are not all here. We are familiar with physical existence and accept it as being here. When I was on the other side, this life was just a sad, sad joke. I'm very unhappy with it.

You are rooted in this system. If you stop breathing while you're on the other side, you won't be back. It's as simple as that. I had a choice over this the first couple of times I went over. I had complete knowledge and there were no blind decisions. I knew exactly what was involved, but for some reason, I chose to come back. I was given the opportunity to knowingly choose.

The main reason for coming back was my attachment to people. I was so attached to the idea of my death generating a sense of loss in them. Come to the fork in the road, I'll go back and see. I didn't know what was going to happen. In one sense you have completely resolved all questions over there. You come back out of a sense of duty, which is generated out of being here. It is not native to that condition. I was still alive here, so I still would have died here. Had I ceased living here, the sense of duty would have evaporated. It is only generic to this condition. When you are in that condition, you are true to it also. When you are on the fence and the life force and health is good, you tend to come back. You think you have a choice, but you probably don't. What makes us want to come here to physical existence is a real question. All I can tell you is that we are incurable nebshits! I can remember with sane clarity one experience in this lifetime of being on the other side. It was very... all encompassing. I could talk about aspects of it for hours. It only contained about fourteen hours. It was an experience of our being to experience that has been uncommon to me, so I often return to it in my wondering. When I was there I was at peace. At first, to say that I couldn't believe it only suggests the force that it had. It was peace. Now I knew a man, now here's a switch, he had a scratch for every itch—and that was me. But I was there, so in time I believed it, remembering that the time experience on that side is totally different.

Once you've had this experience, you come back with one apparently unreduceable experience. You realize that all you are here, is made by being here, and it is to answer to this dimension alone. When you come to this experience, you will recoil in fear. If you are forced into it many times, you will come to a condition of being unfrightened by the unanswered. You come to a state where you accept the fact that this is the limit of your present capacity to know, and are not threatened by what you know is knowable, but not by you now.

I wouldn't object to success in the world if it wasn't at the cost of inner accomplishment. My answer is to know the Self. You see people chasing cars and status and money and all the rest of it, and the more they get the more they want, and there's no end to it. It means they have mislabeled their urges. They are looking in the wrong direction. What they don't know is that they want to understand their own inner workings. They are like children and look outside for internal answers.

A side of human nature has to be able to go out, work, and accomplish, I've been unable to do this. You can't be as one-sided as me and have a great deal of relief, although I have about as much relief as anyone, but on the other side of the fence, internally instead of externally. People are always at war within but just don't know it. I'm different in that I've faced this war and had my day in the sun. Once you've had a day in the sun, your system will not accept any other answer. The things that satisfy me now—a simple room, a few pegs to hang my belongings on, would send most people living in the success mode into the depths of depression. To me it is being free, free from having to chase things.

# Q&A with Jim Burns
# 2006

❦

*Question: What are the most important things to do on a path?*

The key to the path is threefold. The first is free association. The second is holding awareness through all states of consciousness [i.e., going to sleep slowly]. And the last is dream analysis.

*Question: How does one go within?*

The direct route to learning the answer to that question: Learn to go to sleep very slowly. Don't break from consciousness to sleep consciousness. That is how I learned. I stumbled on that... Talk about the grace of God.

*Question: What am I supposed to be doing while I am going to sleep slowly? Am I supposed to be reliving the day, watching, talking to myself....what am I supposed to be doing?*

In the beginning, you have to learn how to clear your mind of daily concerns. You have to take them one at a time until they die a death of their own. This is what permits you once you accomplish this. This permits you and brings you to the edge. And you realize that if you try, you can take your daily consciousness once changed into sleep and not lose track of it. Once you have accomplished this, you never leave the waking state consciousness again. It carries into all things, fundamentally a clear-headed sharp capacity into insight into all matters regardless of what they are in the mental aspect, which is part of everything. That is the goal. It was built into you and buried by misconception, but once you try to bring it back to life, it will have a life of its own.

*Question: How does one develop their intuition?*

If you mean by intuition, how do you develop the ability to get answers to questions... Well, once you learn how to go to the edge of consciousness and sit there you will find that information comes and that information comes is key in perfection to what you were dealing with whether you know it or not at that moment. The secret to that is realizing that the machine within makes no mistakes. You start out and it seems like gibberish and it is since you weren't taught the function was there and you weren't taught how to use it.

*Question: What is the best path to enlightenment?*

Above. Your inner self seeks nothing else but to be known, and when you find your inner self you will know what illumination means.

*Question: What is the most valuable piece of advice you can give?*

Learn to go to sleep slowly and learn to wake up slowly. When you practice that and put effort into it, you will carry common garden variety consciousness in an uninterrupted flow night or day, sleep or awake.

And one other thing: find someone to share it with. You can't go it alone.

*Question: But you did it alone?*

I wouldn't send the devil down that road.

One tragic flaw in my system is that you have to have someone feed you since it consumes all of your time. When I needed a break, I would go out and play with the kids on the street growing up.

*Question: Do you have any insight into Christianity?*

God help anyone who doesn't. The damn thing about the Catholic Church is that they have all of the answers but none of the questions. All they are interested in is pomp, circumstance, influence, and money.

*Question: But you said something about Christ once?*

The story is don't do as I say, do as I do.

*Question: Meaning, do what Christ did not what he said?*

Right.

*Question: How does Christ fit into anything?*

I'd have to get into cosmology and metaphysics. Your inner self—your intuition and inner illumination—is the Christ condition and is in every human being. And they don't know it since they have been trained away from the only guide there is...them.

*Question: What is the function of awareness?*

That question is a hot potato. Your existence in this plane and any other plane has only one constant...your awareness.

*Question: What does that mean?*

It begs the question of what is reality? Reality is your awareness of it.

*Question: Can you elaborate?*

I'm thinking... Christ said that until you become as a child you cannot know the face of God.

*Question: What does that mean?*

You have to wrestle with the question: is life actually doable? It is if you are lucky and you are given grace to get through the next minute — and know how to reach for it and find it — you at least have a decent chance of making it. But there are no absolute guarantees, you can get hit by a truck and it is good night Alice.

*Question: Is there life after death?*

Is there ever.

*Question: What is it?*

A condition of self in a completely and totally loving existence, which is what the remark is meant by until you become as a child — a lucky child.

*Question: Is there reincarnation?*

I'm afraid so. Generally speaking, people are terrified of reincarnation since the thought of going through this again is the description of a nightmare. When you go to the other side, there is perfect knowledge, and you realize that the purpose of reincarnation is to come back time and time again to amass perfect knowledge about existence in this world.

*Question: What do you know about meditation?*

I know all there is to know.

*Question: Which is?*

I stumbled on the meditation in my mid-teens when I was laying on a bed. Arms and feet straight out and it occurred to me to let my mind wander. I didn't know what I was trying to do or trying to get to, but I knew it was the thing to do. I did this for hours until I began to get familiar with the inner workings of consciousness in that state—awake and not asleep. Ultimately, I went to the top of the mountain and I knew what it was that I set out to learn. It was a one time thing, I did it once and there was no need to do it again. All of this is laid out in a matrix, based in ideas that came earlier, that the mind had many facets. I hoped that if it did that God would show me the way to get my mind fully functional. Meditation was one of the ways of completion—fulfillment.

I spent tens of hundreds of hours thinking through anything that came to me, whether it made me uncomfortable or upset. I found the source of it and it was gone. The last straw for [name withheld] was that I said to him that I have answered all of my questions, which is true.

*Question: What about the meditation? I heard you talk about the time you relaxed your big toe up through your body until you saw a bright light.*

That was a couple of years after the mountain experience. A situation by the way which is how you start meditation. Take the tension out of every muscle one at a time. That is how you bring on an altered state, which will bring you the fulfillment of the desire to get what you are going to get done.

The other meditation I had that was very instrumental was I did the same thing in which I was aware of a tall floor lamp that was lit but had no shade—just a socket and a light bulb. Suddenly, I was consumed by the light, and I became a spirit body and went from the light from the building I was in, to the other side. When I got there I met Jesus. He asked me something but I can't remember exactly what. But his response was that I was like everyone else who went there feeling that everything that went wrong was my fault. He said you didn't have perfect knowledge and without it none of it was your fault. He also stated that perfect knowledge is what we are trying to arrive at. Perfect knowledge is illumination.

I am remembering that far more clearly than I have for fifty or sixty years. When I left there, I knew what I was getting into. I had the choice to stay or come back. I chose to come back and knew it was going to be murder.

*Question: Why did you come back?*

The only thing that ever comes to mind about that, is that I just thought I would come back and try to help out.

*Question: I'm glad you did.*

The truth is quite a few people have been.

*Question: What is the inner self made of?*

Awareness.

*Question: That's what I thought...*

It is the only constant in existence. Life in consciousness is an ever changing thing. You are always learning, but the key is that your condition of learning and being aware is what awareness is all about.

*Question: What do you mean by that?*

Just what I said.

The goal is to be peacefully and rejoicefully aware and awake in common garden variety consciousness. It is the goal we all seek to achieve. If you work at the things I am saying, if you can find the time, you cannot miss getting there. If you don't have the time, you are finished and it eats time. It is the biggest reason why no one ever said much to anyone about it since once they realize that all the time they have and all the effort they can stand to put out is eaten by paying the bills. I was carried along first by my family and then by social security disability. There is where I got the time. I knew one thing the whole way through: that I dare not waste one second.

*Question: Anything else you want to say?*

WWWWhew!

# Biography

Jim Burns was born in 1931 in the Squirrel Hill section of Pittsburgh. The son of a prominent Irish-American attorney, he completed Catholic primary and secondary schools, followed by liberal arts studies at the University of Pittsburgh and the University of Miami at Coral Gables. He expressed his aptitude for complex thinking in his interests in philosophy and psychology, and in his youthful employment in his father's law firm. He also showed a fondness for intricate processes of a different sort in his periodic work as a service station attendant and mechanic. Despite Jim's keen intelligence and varied interests, he was afflicted by both physical handicaps and mental illness that prevented him from completing his studies and pursuing a full-time career.

In the 1960s, an astute psychiatrist became impressed with Jim's intelligence, imagination, and verbal skills. Hoping that Jim would find companionship among like-minded intuitive people, he referred him to an organization called the A.R.E. (Association for Research and Enlightenment, founded by America's "sleeping prophet" Edgar Cayce), and Jim became its enthusiastic member for over ten years. Jim met many friends in the A.R.E. with whom he explored the inner workings of various occult systems and world religions. It was an A.R.E. friend who introduced Jim to T.A.T. founder Richard

Rose in the early 1980s, and subsequently Jim was an invited guest at many T.A.T. gatherings in Pittsburgh and West Virginia. Independent of T.A.T., Jim has continuously shared his unique insights with many people in the Pittsburgh area interested in his eclectic blend of psychology and esoteric self-study.

# Index

## A
abuse 65
A.R.E. (Assocaiton for Research and Enlightenment) 11, 83, 119

## C
chemistry 67, 90, 99
childhood 13, 25, 57 – 65
child-like state 64
Christ 77, 101, 111 – 112

## D
death 65, 95, 104, 106, 113
dream(s) 44, 48 – 49, 91, 109
drugs 71, 103

## E
ego 18, 27, 32 – 38, 52, 63, 67, 84, 92 – 93
ego death 32, 38, 92
enlightenment 110

## F
family 26, 75, 91
fantasy (fantasies) 19, 23, 58, 59, 65, 81, 88, 95
fear 33, 43, 70, 100, 107
free association 41, 48, 54, 88, 109
Freud (Freudian) 9, 35, 50, 65, 67, 70
fulfillment 19, 29, 59, 92, 102, 104, 114 – 115

## G
God 57 – 58, 64, 83, 112
guilt 33, 39, 58, 60

- those disconnected from themselves know how to hurt others in uncanny way. pg 62
- a street smart person → to a cult. (circles of logic)
- ~~E~~Worst frustration = not being allowed to love
- 82  If true to yourself = alone. Japan = hard.
- How does your body respond when it meets another ⊕/⊖. Bring body response to C & hold it that